THE

ROMANCE OF AMERICAN COLONIZATION

BOOKS BY WILLIAM ELLIOT GRIFFIS.

THE ROMANCE OF DISCOVERY: A Thousand Years of Exploration and the Unveiling of Continents. 305 pages. With five full-page illustrations by Frank T. Merrill. Cloth, gilt top. 12mo. $1.50.

THE ROMANCE OF AMERICAN COLONIZATION: How the Foundation Stones of Our History were Laid. 295 pages. With five full-page illustrations by Frank T. Merrill. Cloth, gilt top. 12mo. $1.50.

THE ROMANCE OF CONQUEST: The Story of American Expansion through Arms and Diplomacy. 316 pages. With five full-page illustrations by Frank T. Merrill. Cloth, gilt top. 12mo. $1.50.

THE PATHFINDERS OF THE REVOLUTION: A Story of the Great March into the Wilderness and Lake Region of New York in 1779. 316 pages. With five full-page illustrations by W. F. Stecher. Cloth. 12mo. $1.50.

IN THE MIKADO'S SERVICE: A Story of Two Battle Summers in China. 361 pages. With five full-page illustrations by W. F. Stecher. Cloth. 12mo. $1.50.

WASHINGTON'S FIRST COMMAND.

THE ROMANCE OF AMERICAN COLONIZATION

HOW THE FOUNDATION STONES OF OUR HISTORY WERE LAID

BY

WILLIAM ELLIOT GRIFFIS

MEMBER OF THE AMERICAN HISTORICAL ASSOCIATION
AUTHOR OF "THE MIKADO'S EMPIRE," "BRAVE LITTLE HOLLAND"
"THE PILGRIMS IN THEIR THREE HOMES," "THE
ROMANCE OF DISCOVERY," ETC.

ILLUSTRATED BY

FRANK T. MERRILL

BOSTON AND CHICAGO

W. A. WILDE & COMPANY

THE ROMANCE OF AMERICAN COLONIZATION.

TO THE

"𝔅𝔯𝔬𝔱𝔥𝔢𝔯 𝔅𝔬𝔶𝔰"

STANTON AND JOHN

MAY THEY INHERIT THE VIRTUES

AND AVOID THE VICES

OF THEIR

ENGLISH ANCESTORS

PREFACE.

THE foundations of the American Commonwealth, as laid by Divine Providence, are broader and deeper than the average writer of our national history seems to have perceived. Our country is not a new England. It is a new and better Europe, dominated by that kind of Christianity which is all the purer because of freedom from political control. To the making of the nation many peoples contributed by sending their sons and daughters with varied gifts of race and temperament, as well as with faith, moral fibre, ideas, and experience.

In "The Romance of American Colonization," omitting military matters, the story from Sir Walter Raleigh to July 4, 1776, is briefly told. Less stress has been laid upon mere political enactments and the doings of kings and princes, and more upon the work of the people themselves. The purpose has rather been to show what the real builders of the nation have done.

It is not forgotten that Swiss, German, Dutch, French, Walloon, Scandinavian, Welsh, Irish, and Scottish, as well as English, helped to make our country. Christian and

Jew, Catholic and Protestant, political and free church-men, Puritan and Lutheran, believers and skeptics, the Indian and the Negro, have borne each his part in the making of colonial America.

If it appears in this book that to the Middle region is given an importance equal to the Eastern or Southern, that our fathers took most of their political precedents from a republic and not from a monarchy, that our general procedure is adapted from democratic rather than aristocratic communities, that our religion is continued from free rather than political churches, that the emigration of the Scotch-Irish exerted an influence second to none other, that the Catholics have been a nobly conservative force, and that in the American composite the continental as well as the insular elements have been potent leaven for freedom and righteousness, it is because the facts seem to warrant the statements made.

What a wonderful process of sifting and filtering, of being poured from vessel to vessel, was that among the nations of northern Europe, which gave us under God the mother-liquid out of which has crystallized the republic of the United States of America !

W. E. G.

ITHACA, N.Y., June, 1898.

TABLE OF CONTENTS.

9

ILLUSTRATIONS.

11

THE ROMANCE OF AMERICAN COLONIZATION.

CHAPTER I.

WHAT IS A COLONY?

WHAT is a colony?
Down at the roots, the idea of a colony is that of a company of people away from their old home, who are cultivating the soil. True colonists are first of all farmers. There may be sailors, soldiers, priests, political rulers; but unless there are tillers of the soil who expect to make the new country their home, there is no true colony. A garrison, a body of traders, a governor and his staff of officers, do not make a colony. People who emigrate, but expect to stay awhile and then go back home again, will never make a settlement that will grow into a state. A true colony begins when men make the earth on which they dwell support them.

There were not a few colonies in the ancient world. The mythology of many nations teaches that their ancestors grew out of the soil, but history shows that they came from other countries.   Asia and Europe were colonized as well as America.   The story of the colonization of Korea, Japan, and India is quite well, and that of China fairly, known.

The most ancient voyage of discovery mentioned by the classic poets and myth-makers is that of the ship *Argo*, before the Trojan War.   Under command of Jason, the Argonauts sailed to Colchis on the Euxine Sea to recover the Golden Fleece, which was guarded by a sleepless dragon.   Hercules, Theseus, Castor, Pollux, and Orpheus were among the famous heroes in the crew.   How they tamed the fire-breathing bulls, slew the dragon, sowed its teeth, won the fleece, and escaped the sirens is told in the lovely Grecian fairy lore.   In plain prose, all this means that after a rough voyage and many adventures a band of colonists broke up the hard soil with the plough, sowed their seed, suffered many terrors, but persevered until the golden fleece, in the form of a harvest of ripe grain, covered the landscape.   They succeeded in colonization and then began trade.   Our American history, though real, is a much more wonderful story, and the golden fleece of our national prosperity a thousand-fold richer.

Greece was one of the first countries in Europe to be civilized, because it was nearest to the old seats of civilization in Egypt and Syria. Through the Trojan War the Greeks became acquainted with Asia and its riches. When the Hellenic states became overcrowded, colonization began by public act. The poor and the discontented, among whom there were many dangerous characters, who were yet brave and enterprising, were shipped to other lands to form Greater Greece. These led to the enterprises which lined the coast of Asia Minor with settlements that grew into rich and flourishing cities. Shut up by their mountains on the north, the Greeks were free upon the sea. Sailing in every direction, they located in the Crimea, upon the coasts of Italy, and even in France, Spain, and Africa.

The emigrants took from their old homes fire kindled on the city hearthstone, and remembered the traditions of heroism and religion taught them by their fathers and mothers. A typical Greek city on the Mediterranean lay midway between the deep blue sea in front and the wheat fields, orchards, and groves on land, and often in rich valley or at the mouth of a river. Reared at first of wood, it became in time a glorious mass of brick and marble.

With agriculture, industry, and commerce, there grew up a Greek world. These colonists, looking with reverence upon the mother country, still regarded themselves as Greeks. Their language was one. Their common book was Homer. Their method of government was federal. The several states were represented in the Congress called the Amphictyonic League. At the public games any Greek, from the Black Sea region to the Iberian peninsula guarded by the Pillars of Hercules, could contend with full rights. Glorious was the history of the Greek colonists during a thousand years.

The Romans developed colonial enterprises on a grand scale. From them we get the word "colony," though we must add Greek to get "colonize" and "colonization." A colony was a collection of *coloni* or farmers in a new land. The root-idea of a colonist was that he was a *colonus*, or husbandman who tilled the soil and dwelt upon it. The words "colony," "cultivate," "cult," and "culture" have all the same root, which, back in the ancient Sanskrit tongue, is probably *kal*, which means to drive. As the root-idea of father is that of protector, of mother manager, and of daughter milker, so in that of colonist we have the picture of a ploughman behind his oxen turning up the soil for food.

The first Roman colonies were made up of soldiers who garrisoned the conquered or hostile territory. When Italy became overcrowded, colonies were founded for the benefit of the poor of Rome. This was a sort of ancient and permanent "Fresh-air Fund." When the empire required large armies to occupy its vast domain, there were great numbers of veterans, for whom it must provide. These old soldiers were not pensioned in money, as in our modern history; for Rome was rich in land rather than in cash. So it was after our Revolutionary War, when the United States was very poor in coin, but very rich in territory. The old Continentals were paid not in gold and silver, but in land warrants. The American *coloni* helped largely in building up what was then called the Great West.

The Roman colony was thus a foundation for the benefit of veteran soldiers who had served out their time in the army. These colonists retained their citizenship, while receiving their lands by lot. When the empire extended from Britain to Persia and from Germany to the African deserts, colonies were very numerous. They were of various grades, but every district settled was considered an integral part of the empire. In some colonies settlers enjoyed all, but in others only a few privileges of Roman citizenship. Veterans usually settled on the soil allotted to them and married, and their children and descendants grew up, becoming citizens both of the particular state and of the empire. As a rule, the central government at Rome appointed their ablest men as colonial governors, but their tenure of office was limited, lest through personal influence they might grow too powerful. The chief feature of the Roman system, that of centralization, was carefully preserved in order to prevent colonies from becoming independent.

This is the system, in an improved form, which the British government has so largely copied, especially since the American Revolutionary War, which taught much wisdom. Many of the English governors sent to rule our fathers were weak, foolish, or unworthy men; but now extreme care is taken in London to send the ablest men to Canada, India, South Africa, Australia, and other colonies. They are also moved about from country to country, so as to keep power centralized in England. The Irishman Sir Hercules Robinson, one of the best of Great Britain's colonial governors, of whose death in October, 1897, we read as we revise this chapter, governed well no fewer than six British colonies on four continents. Nevertheless, signs are not wanting that the idea of federation, so splendidly demonstrated in American history, will yet become the rule, and the British United States take the place of the United Kingdom and her colonies.

Grandly the Roman colonies fulfilled their mission. To-day, after more than twelve hundred years from the fall of the Roman empire, we see that some of the richest associations of history are with colonies. When St. Paul sailed from the seaport of Troas in Asia to introduce Christian civilization in

Europe, he preached the gospel first at Philippi, which, as St. Luke, the historian of the Book of Acts, notes, was a colony, or, as the Geneva version says, a place to which people went from Rome to live. The name of another Roman colony in Britain, on the Lind River, has descended to us in that of a city and also of Lincoln, one of the greatest of our presidents. In the geography of the Roman empire no name is more frequently found than that of Colonia, unless we except Augusta and Castra. Besides the term signifying that the place was a colony, there was some other name given from circumstances attending the settlement. Just as " castra," or camp, becomes changed into " caster " as in Lancaster, Cæsarea into Jersey, Julius Cæsar into Julich or Gulick, and Cæsar Augustus into Saragossa, so the word " colonia " has suffered curious changes, as we see in English " coln " and " colony " and in Cologne on the Rhine.

In the Roman as well as in the Greek colonial system, the idea of close connection with and dependence upon the mother country was always maintained. The governing corporation of each Roman colony was dependent upon that of Rome. The idea was that the colony was always to be a part of the nation and empire.

This description separates the Roman or Greek colony entirely from that of a simple migration or

wandering of a people from the old ancestral seats,
into a new country or continent; as, for example,
when the Asiatic tribes that came to inhabit North
America forgot their old homes. When the high-
landers on the steppes of North Asia, known in
history as Scythians, Huns, Turks, Tartars, or
Mongols, in various ages invaded the southern
countries, they also retained little or no connection
with their ancestral lands. Indeed, uncivilized people, that is, people who have no writing, quickly
forget their past. Whether it be the New Englanders who go down into the mountains of Kentucky,
or the Normans who descend from Scandinavia into
France, they forget their fathers. Illiteracy means
darkness as to history. Life without letters is death.
We do not, therefore, speak of the westward migration of the Celts as far as Ireland, the advance of
the Teutonic or of the Gothic nations into western
or southern Europe, as movements of colonists; for
they kept no remembrance of the land they left
behind.

During the middle ages, the Italians sent out
bodies of men into various parts of the Mediterranean, who extended Venetian and Genoese trade
and commerce in subject or neighbor lands. Various companies of Lombards, and other Italians,
went also into northern Europe. They became
the money-changers of the nations beyond the

Alps, introducing financial customs and enterprises. Yet these can hardly be called true colonists.

In modern times, we must award first honors of colonization to the Portuguese and Spaniards; for the former had planted colonies, some a century old, in Brazil, Africa, and Asia, and the latter in South America, Mexico, and the West Indies, before the Englishmen obtained foothold on any continent beyond Europe. Yet, let us note at once how different these were—the Spanish and Portuguese—from the English and Dutch methods and results. The two nations of the Iberian peninsula did, indeed, lead the modern European states in replenishing and subduing newly discovered continents, yet in neither case were these enterprises begun by a movement of the people. The King of Spain, considering America as his private property, wished to establish one great empire in Europe, and another beyond the Atlantic, so that when united under his own crown, these should be grander in area and splendor than the old Roman empire itself. With this purpose in view, he sent out noblemen of high rank with princely salaries, who led their personal followers after them. So, also, did Portugal in Brazil and the East, and France in Canada and Louisiana. It was the old Roman way over again, without any improvement. The story of the early Spanish explorers in America has been already told in our previous volume, entitled " The Romance of Discovery."

In the case of the British and Dutch colonists, the spirit and method were entirely different. The people went first. The dignitaries followed afterward. The colonies which now form the United States were, for the most part, the results of movements among the English, Scottish, Irish, Welsh, Huguenot, Walloon, and German people, who were dissatisfied either with the kind of government under which they lived, or the religion which politicians tried to force upon them. They were not contented, for the very good reason that their consciences had been enlightened. They could not live happily under the sort of church and state which then existed. They longed for more freedom. Coming to the new continent of America, they obtained what they sought. Some, indeed, — Dutch, Swedes, Swiss, English, — without any grievances at home, were moved by love of adventure or were tempted by hopes of wealth to be got in the fisheries, the fur trade, the supposed gold mines, by rearing silkworms, or in developing the wonderful resources of the new land.

English colonization was begun by the English people. At first these pioneers who had crossed the sea were ignored or neglected by their government. Only when the colonies began to prosper

did royalty pay much attention to them. Becoming
rich, they offered a tempting field for taxation and
the filling of the British coffers. Then king and
parliament joined in a scheme to tax the American
colonists in the Roman way, which was something
which men of Dutch and British descent would not
stand. The ancient doctrine, first formulated by
the Netherlanders and later by the English, was
" No taxation without consent." They who pay
the taxes must first vote them.

It was not until after the Revolutionary War that
the British government fully formulated a colonial
policy like that of the ancient Roman empire, but
with modern improvements added because of experience with America. Such a policy, wisely carried
out, has been best for both the colonists and aborigines. It often happens that the first discoverers,
explorers, and settlers are little better than pirates
and robbers, who take land as they please, caring
nothing for the rights of inferior races already on
the soil. The British colonists in Africa, Australia,
New Zealand, India, and other parts of the world
have found that all the land which they had conquered, occupied, or bought in large quantities from
the natives for guns, beads, wire, shovels, a looking-
glass, or a piece of red cloth was not wholly their
own. These have had to yield their claims to
those of the British crown. Having learned wis-

dom from her mistakes in dealing with the American colonies, Great Britain has become the mother of many nations.

In the sixteenth and seventeenth centuries, the first object of a patriotic Englishman or Dutchman was to humble Spain. The monarchy that then owned America was the dominating power threatening all Europe. The two small countries which crippled and impoverished Spain became the two most successful colonizers the modern world has seen. In American history, the term " colony " has come into our speech from the Dutch. In Virginia, the Carolinas, and Massachusetts the settlements were all called " plantations," but in New Netherland " colonies."

CHAPTER II.

SIR WALTER RALEIGH led the way in awakening the English mind to colonial enterprise and even in attempting himself to plant colonies in the region of Virginia. Although these first ventures failed, Raleigh will not be forgotten by Americans.

Woman's aid helped mightily to make America. As Isabella first encouraged Columbus, so Queen Elizabeth favored Raleigh. In 1578 she granted the first charter for English colonization on the North American continent. The name, Virginia, which she gave, though now restricted to a single state, included all the land which on July 4, 1776, became the United States of America. In this first charter the number of the councillors was thirteen, — as many as the states which formed the Union. How often does Divine Providence smite human superstition, in making great events, rich in happiness for mankind, occur on Friday, and how often is the number thirteen honored!

Although the Cabots sailed and made landfall under the Tudors, yet these rulers were not destined

to plant the Germanic race or the English people
in America.   This honor was reserved for the worst
dynasty that disgraced the throne of Great Britain.
On the 10th of April, 1606, King James Stuart put
his signature to the patent which chartered two
companies, the London and the Plymouth, bestow-
ing on them in equal proportions the territory in
America, including adjacent islands, lying between
the thirty-fourth and forty-fifth degrees of north
latitude.   For the first five years the people were to
live together, holding common land, property, and
food.

China, gold, and spice were still the lure of colonists.   To show how the minds of every one, king
and people, were possessed with the ideas of finding
a water-route to China and of getting gold out of
the soil, it was stipulated that one-fifth of the precious metal found should belong to the king.   All
waterways near the colony were to be explored, in
order to find a short and easy way to the Pacific
Ocean.   Although the charter was published in
England, the instructions of the king were put in a
sealed box and with much mystery kept secret.
They were not made public until the colonists
reached Virginia.

One may wonder why Englishmen could be
tempted to leave home.   Their little country had
then only about four millions of people, most of

whom lived in the southern tier of counties, from which a majority of the settlers came.

In the year 1606, however, times were hard and food was dear. It was not dreamed then that England could ever support a population of nearly forty millions of souls, which is now done through improved agriculture and commerce. Furthermore, after Queen Elizabeth in 1585 took up the cause of the Dutch United States and sent an army to help the Netherlanders against Spain, there had been tens of thousands of English soldiers, with officers, contractors, and merchants, in the Low Countries, but now in 1606 the war between Holland and Spain was over. Already the peace negotiations, which were to result in a truce of eleven years, were under way. Thousands of British soldiers were thus thrown out of employment. When paid off and discharged at home, they were idlers waiting for a job. Not only had the military business, with its contracts and trade, helped to make England rich, but the one hundred thousand people, mostly skilled workmen or intelligent business men, driven out of the Belgic Netherlands by Alva, had introduced those manufactures which were to make England rich. There was temporary distress, however, for the supply of breadstuffs had fallen short, because the landowners were turning their fields into sheep pastures, to raise wool instead of wheat. On account of this great change in agriculture, from plough land to meadow, which left harrow and hoe rusty for want of use, a large army of farm laborers found themselves with nothing to do.

So all eyes were turned to America as a continent where work was not only plenty, but gold was abundant. The common notion, as shown in the popular plays of the time in the theatre and in the books, was that the American rivers "ran down their golden sands," that nuggets were as plentiful as marbles and the yellow metal more common than red copper in England. Furthermore, lively young men believed that among the "diggings," there was "no more law than conscience and not too much of either."

In our time, Klondike explains to us the eagerness of these seventeenth-century Englishmen to try their fortunes in the American wilderness. Even the gold-hunting Spaniards, though they chased phantoms, seem, after all, not so very different from the men of to-day, who, in the hope of wealth or for love of adventure or "the danger's self to lure alone," will hazard health and life even in icy regions.

With so many men out of work and population pressing upon the food-supply, Virginia seemed "the door which God had opened to England."

The London Company had no trouble in getting young men to go out as "planters," and in this enterprise of 1606 there were neither wives nor children. It was a company of bachelors, like a military battalion. Of the one hundred and five colonists, more than half called themselves "gentlemen"; that is, men without any manual trade or skilled employment, younger sons who had not inherited property and who were not accustomed to handle tools or do the downright hard work necessary, in all first attempts, to make the soil produce food. The others were laborers, tradesmen, and mechanics, with two surgeons and a chaplain.

On the 19th of December, 1606, three ships moored at Blackwall, London, where are now the East India docks, took on their human cargo. The largest ship was the *Susan Constant* of one hundred tons, Captain Christopher Newport, commander and fleet-captain; the *God-speed* of forty tons, Captain Bartholomew Gosnold, commander; and the *Discovery* of twenty tons, Captain John Ratcliffe. The total tonnage of these three little ships was less than that of the *Mayflower* of later days and of many a canal boat of to-day. There were thirty-nine men in the crews and one hundred and five colonists, of whom seventy-one were in the first, fifty-two in the second, and twenty in the third ship — one hundred and forty-four in all. Farewells and salutes being over, the little squadron sailed down the Thames, but when in the English Channel contrary winds detained them until New Year's Day. Then they moved westward across the Atlantic along the old route to the West Indies and up the coast into Chesapeake Bay. After a nearly four months' voyage, with their new home in sight, they opened the box of royal instructions, finding that the councillors named were Wingfield, Gosnold, Smith, Newport, Ratcliffe, Martin, and Kendell. The first three of these, and probably others, had seen military service in the armies of the Dutch republic.

Three days afterwards they landed and planted a cross, naming the place, after the Prince of Wales, Cape Henry. The other cape at the mouth of Chesapeake Bay, they called Cape Charles, after the future king of that name. Anchoring the next day, they gratefully named the place Point Comfort. They sailed up the river, in the beautiful time of flowers, landing in May upon a peninsula. The name of their king was given to the river and to the town which they founded.

Knowing that they were surrounded by natives who might be hostile and remembering how Raleigh's colony had perished, they at once began building a fort and laying out James City. Captain John Smith, then twenty-eight years of age and a man of splendid abilities, showed himself at once a leader. China was in fancy still near. Smith and Newport, with twenty-three men, took the small boat and started on a tour of exploration up the river, going beyond the site of Richmond. Among other wonderful things seen, was a boy, ten years old, with yellow hair and light skin, who may have been a descendant of one of the Roanoke settlers. Indian tradition declared that several of the survivors had been adopted into the tribes. In later days a small band of gray-eyed savages were found on the North Carolina coast, who claimed that their ancestors were white men.

Smith's exploring party returned on the 27th of May, and found that the natives had attacked the settlers, but had been driven off by Wingfield, who had more than once shown his valor in the Netherlands. Two men had been killed and ten wounded. When, on the 15th of June, the fort was finished, the chaplain, Rev. Robert Hunt, held what was perhaps the first public worship in English held in America, and administered the communion. On the next day, Monday, Captain Newport sailed homeward in the largest ship, *Susan Constant*, which was loaded with timber and mineral specimens, some, no doubt, expected to contain precious metal.

Provisions had been left for three months, but

life in the colony was not very happy. Disappointed in not finding gold, unused to the hard work which was necessary, surrounded by hostile savages, and divided among themselves, their many troubles were further increased by the malarious climate of the region in which they had made their settlement.

Fever was epidemic. Quinine, not discovered by the Jesuit missionaries of Peru until 1638, was unknown either as medicine, stimulant, or groceries. When autumn began, nearly one-half of the colonists had died, and many of the remainder were ill. Hardly more than a score of able-bodied men attended the sick and kept guard.

With cool weather there was improvement, especially since they were now able to dwell in log houses. They also built a church, and the energetic Captain John Smith obtained supplies of grain from the Indians. He was captured by the savages, but was released after a few weeks' imprisonment on promising to give the Indians two great guns and a grindstone. Reaching Jamestown, he found only forty men living.

Captain Newport returned from England early in January with more settlers, but within a week afterward the fort and several of the houses were destroyed by fire. On a visit to Powhatan, the Indian chief, Captains Newport and Smith obtained supplies of food and exchanged pledges of mutual friendship. An Indian lad was taken to England, while the English boy Thomas Savage stayed with Powhatan and became very useful afterwards as an interpreter. The ship, loaded with iron ore, sassafras, cedar posts, and walnut boards, sailed homeward on the 10th of April.

Meanwhile the colonists began to rebuild James City. They cast their seed into the ground, hoping for generous crops, but while waiting for the corn to grow, what with fever and insufficient food, about half their number died. To the great joy of the survivors, the *Phœnix* arrived with fresh provisions and seventy settlers. Sailing again on June 22, she took back a cargo of cedar wood.

Smith now began in earnest the work of exploration. He went up the Chesapeake Bay and into its tributaries. He opened trade with the natives, and on a second expedition, toward the end of July, he reached the head of the bay. Here he was entertained by a party of Iroquois warriors, whose great forest republic of five federated nations extended from the Hudson River to Niagara Falls. The map drawn by Captain John Smith has been the basis of nearly all others made since. It was even used as an authority in 1873, in settling the boundary dispute between the states of Virginia and Maryland. When elected president of the council, Smith brought order and discipline into the settlement.

Another reinforcement of seventy colonists arrived, among whom were Francis West, the brother of Lord Delaware; a lady, Mrs. Thomas Forest, and her maid, Ann Burras. Before the end of the year Ann was married to John Laydon, and the first wedding in Virginia was celebrated.

Better far than a batch of the average immigrants, was the reinforcement of some German and Polish mechanics, brought over to manufacture glass. These Germans were the first of a great company that have contributed powerfully to build up the industry and commerce of Virginia, — "the mother of states and statesmen." There still stands on the east side of Timber Neck Bay, on the north side of the York River, a stone chimney, with a mighty fireplace nearly eight feet wide, built by these Germans.

The directors of the London Company were excessively greedy for gold. When Captain Newport left England again, they required of him a pledge to fulfil at least two of four conditions. He was not to return without a nugget of gold, the news of the discovery of a passage to China, one of the settlers of the lost company of Sir Walter Raleigh, or freight in his vessel equal in value to the cost of the expedition, which was two thousand pounds sterling. If he failed in all of these conditions, then the Jamestown colonists were to be left to shift for themselves. Perhaps Lord Bacon had these men in his eye, when he wrote in 1625 : "The principal thing that hath been the destruction of most plantations hath been the base and hasty drawing of profit in the first years."

The captain tried hard to redeem his promise. Having brought costly presents to Powhatan, he wasted much time in the ceremony of coronation, and strained every nerve to get a valuable cargo. At that time there was great demand in England for naval stores, but all that could be done was to load the ship with some pitch tar, glass, and iron ore. When smelted, the metal yielded twenty dollars a ton, or, in our values, about eighty dollars.

Although two hundred colonists were in Jamestown, yet almost the only man of vigor was Smith, who soon became the head of the government. He cheered the industrious, and the lazy soon found that they must work or starve. Colonial matters improved under his discipline, but for some reason, now unknown, he had to return to England. He never again visited the colony.

Everything seemed to go to pieces after Smith left. Starvation and disease carried off all but about threescore men. Some of these went to live among the Indians, while another party began a settlement some miles from the fort.   When a new ship with reinforcements came in, the entire company, old and new, resolved to return to England. They were actually on the ships, with their faces set homewards, when they were met by a fleet of nine vessels from England, containing nearly five hundred colonists including a considerable number of old veterans who had fought in the Dutch republic.   Once more all rallied to the work of building up a new state.   Perseverance conquered.

CHAPTER III.

TOBACCO, BRIDES, AND BLACK SERVANTS.

THE London Company, in the hope of improving Virginian affairs, had applied for a new charter of privileges, which greatly increased the area of the colony. This was granted on the 23d of May, 1609, and the expedition of nine vessels, as we have seen, sailed from Plymouth on the 1st of June.

The discipline now put in force in the settlement was borrowed from that of the model army organized by Prince Maurice in the Dutch republic, and Sir Thomas Dale, the new governor, made it work admirably. The land was divided, and no more rations were given out from the public storehouse. The church edifice was repaired and the fortifications were improved. A new settlement was planned on Varina Neck at the bend in the James River, called Farrar's Island. The isthmus of this peninsula was called "Dutch Gap," after the glass-makers who set up their furnaces here in 1608. Most Englishmen then made, and uneducated people now make, no distinction between the Dutch and the

Germans, who are politically different people, each with a language of its own. Over two hundred years later, this site was made famous by a canal dug under General Butler's orders and finished by the United States government in 1873.

A new spirit now animated the colony. Men worked cheerfully and gladly. Gardens for hemp, flax, and other seeds were laid out. Under the new code of Dutch laws, "divine, moral, and martial," order and prosperity ruled where disorder and shiftlessness had been. Soon the colony could be called, after a word beloved by Americans, a success.

By June, 1611, when Sir Thomas Gates arrived, there were seven hundred settlers, among whom were women and children, with plenty of provisions besides one hundred cows and other cattle. Gates sent Dale in September to found the town of Henrico, and in December another called Bermuda. This town of "Bermuda Hundred" shows how the old Germanic division of the people into hundreds was early introduced into English America. The old home of the Pilgrim Fathers was in the "Basset-Law Hundred" of Nottingham. The "hundred" still serves in some states as a voting district.

The debt of our English fathers to the Indian is very great, and to the negro even greater. Both

"JOHN ROLFE MARRIED POCAHONTAS, THE DAUGHTER OF POWHATAN."

aided the white man to make America. The Indians, as we shall see, taught the northern colonists culture of corn, woodcraft, natural resources of food, use of the moccasin, snowshoe, birchbark canoe, wampum, and the virtues of tobacco. Where the Indian gave the results of experience, the negro gave his toil. The year 1612 was made famous in Virginia by the systematic culture of this native American plant, discovered by the red and cultivated by the black man.

John Rolfe was the man who first demonstrated the value of the weed and opened a boundless field for slave labor. He also married Pocahontas, the daughter of Powhatan, and thus gained the friendship of the Indians. The couple were married on the 5th of April, 1614, by Rev. Alexander Whitaker. This brought to the colony the good will of the powerful Indian chief, and soon after a treaty was made with the Chickahominy tribe.

These events practically decided the future of the colony and made its future sure. John Rolfe, Pocahontas, and tobacco represent those three elements, — intelligent industry, friendship with neighbors, and a sure income by which permanent success was won. By the steady export of tobacco, commerce was opened with Europe; for Virginia had a commodity always in demand to pay for needed supplies. Through Pocahontas, all present danger from the Indians was removed. Tobacco also furnished a substitute for money and encouraged the colonists to clear the land and begin agriculture, while it attracted new colonists from Europe. In the true sense of the word, the leading men were "planters," and the common English word for a colony was "plantation," as Lord Bacon's essay, written in 1625, shows. Wisely he wrote: "Planting of countries is like planting of woods; for you must make account to lose almost twenty years' profit, and expect your recompense in the end."

The culture of tobacco also influenced Virginia's future history. It made a demand for labor which was unfortunately satisfied by the importation of slaves. It scattered population by preventing its concentration in towns, and thus hindered that close union of the people which, in the Eastern and the Middle colonies, so powerfully promoted education and moulded the character of the people. It was impossible to have in Virginia the system of schools, with the newspaper and the printing press, as in Pennsylvania, or town communities as in Massachusetts, for example. Only a few towns were founded. The population, scattered over a large territory, was composed of rich owners of plantations who, as the soil was quickly exhausted by tobacco under slave labor, added land to land and

pushed farther and farther apart from each other;
while at the same time those who owned no land
were forced into a low social condition and became
" poor white trash," — now in freedom's day so no
longer. Tobacco took the place of money. The
officers of the government and the ministers of
religion were paid and subscriptions made in this
commodity. To help build a house of worship in
Alexandria, Washington subscribed, as I have seen
on the church books, instead of pounds sterling, a
certain number of pounds of tobacco.

Pocahontas visited England with her husband,
but died there in 1617, leaving a son from whom
three of the first families of Virginia trace their
descent. Captain John Smith told many wonderful and romantic stories, mostly about ladies whom
he had met and who had favored him; but it was
not until Pocahontas reached England that he let
any one know of her rescue of him in 1607 from
the war-club of Powhatan.

The year 1619 was also a notable one on account
of the beginning of three great institutions in the
colony, — representative government, homes, and
slavery. Sir George Yeardley arrived on the 19th
of April, and the eleven towns or boroughs — for
there were no counties yet — sent representatives
who met in the chancel of the church building at
Jamestown on July 30. This was the first popu-

lar legislature on the continent of America. At this period only two European states gave the people a share in government. They were Great Britain and the Dutch republic.

Men make a camp, but women a home. White women in the colony, thus far, had been curiosities. Hundreds of bachelors were eager for brides and they stood waiting on the wharf, with their cured tobacco already in their hands, when a ship containing ninety young women hove in sight. The maidens were quickly selected and made wives. Their passage was paid for by the tobacco. There was more marrying within those twenty-four hours than during any one week after the year 1619. It was a red-letter day for the parson. These new daughters of Virginia seemed to like the country and their husbands so well, that they wrote home persuading more rosy-cheeked English girls to come over and to help settle the new country. Promising damsels were not the only white persons to arrive this year, for the company sent over in 1619 numbered nearly twelve hundred new settlers. Among them were boys and girls picked up in the streets of London. These were bound out as apprentices of the planters until they should reach their majority. There were also two hundred disorderly persons or convicts transported to be employed as servants, and thus given a new chance of improvement.

Toward the end of summer of the same year, the sons of Africa appeared as makers of America. There was not much romance in the method of their coming. Yet they had before them, or soon learned of, the example of Joseph sold as a slave by his brethren. Indeed, the black man in America soon appreciated the pathos and meaning of many things in the Bible, such as the year of jubilee, for which their white owners cared little. A ship arrived in want of provisions and traded off twenty African slaves for food. The wickedness of traffic in human bodies had not yet been seen clearly by Christian people. From all the nations of maritime or western Europe, probably without exception, went forth slave-catchers or slave-traders.

Not many black bondsmen came during the first part of the seventeenth century, but in time the system of slavery spread over all the thirteen colonies. These negroes were not the first brought to the new continent, for there were already thousands in the West Indies laboring for the Spaniards. The black man Estevanico had already been with the explorers in Texas and New Mexico. Yet from these first negro bondsmen and those who were imported until 1808, usually called in the South "servants" and "slaves" in the North, the eight millions of our black fellow-citizens in the United States are descended.

Now that it is all over among us, let us see what slavery is. In its origin, slavery is the sign of civilization. In the early wars of the human race, captives were murdered. As men became more civilized, instead of killing their captured enemies, they made them work. The change from massacre to slavery arose probably less from the idea of mercy than of commercial benefit; for as men became less mere fighters, more skilful and productive, they saw the advantage of making bondmen work for them. In the early ages slavery was a benefit to savages, who are naturally lazy. Compelled to toil, their work became an element of progress. Slavery existed among all races that have records, but the Hebrews had laws which mitigated the rigors of bondage; for their slaves became free at the end of seven years, and in the year of jubilee all slaves were emancipated. No ancient book can compare with the Old Testament in the amount and spirit of its language about labor and wages, freedom and slavery. The preamble to the Ten Commandments is the record of a Divine Emancipation Proclamation. Jehovah is the Deliverer. The whole burden of the Old and New Testaments is that of deliverance and release. John Brown's Bible in Charlestown, which I have looked at, and which he marked during many years of study, is powerfully impressive on this theme.

Under the Roman empire, which was a great school of civilization to our barbaric ancestors, the coloni or colonists on the landed estates were *adscripti glebæ*, or enrolled with the soil on which they lived. They were personally free, but could not of their own will leave the lands which they tilled. They were like the *inaka* of Old Japan. In the course of time the actual slaves who had been prisoners of war, or seized to be made bondmen, approached the condition of the coloni. When our Germanic ancestors came into contact with the Roman civilization, their own system was gradually modified, so that instead of slavery came the serfdom of the middle ages. While the feudal system lasted, the condition of most people in Europe was that of serfs, and this social system was not broken up until after the Crusades. These helped powerfully to begin the work of freedom which commerce and industry, under Christian forms, completed; so that in modern times the European people have been free. One late exception was in Russia, where fifty millions of people were little more than beasts of burden, until their emancipation by the Czar Alexander II. in 1861. Then Russian serfs were given the opportunity to become thinking and reasoning men.

So we see that the effect of changing two classes of men, the coloni and the slaves, was to lower the position of the old colonus while it raised that of the agricultural laborer as a whole, thus preparing for modern society through the successive steps of serfdom, feudalism, the Crusades, modern commerce and industry, constitutional governments and republics, where all are perfectly free.

Although the Germanic tribes, including the Anglo-Saxons, held their captives and conquered men in bondage, yet the word "slave" did not come into the English language until very late. Though common in Shakespeare, it is hardly known in the English Bible, occurring only twice. The term did not arise in Europe until about the ninth century, when Slavic men or persons of the Slavonian race were captured by our Germanic ancestors. Then the national appellation of "Slaves" was degraded, by chance or malice, from its original signification of "glory" into that of servitude. The Russian word *slava*, which in our language has come to mean a slave, with all its associations of contempt and woe, means renown or fame. Thus, what is one man's meat is another man's poison. In Asia the same word which in the language on one side of the mountains may mean a god, on the other may mean a devil. One civilization, the Christian, when perfected over all the world, will change all this.

In Old Virginia a planter or house-master always spoke of his negroes as "servants," just as did the

Bible. The Constitution of the United States speaks of "persons held to service or labor," but not of "slaves." It is a potent element in moral progress, when things are called by their right names and the noble word "servant" is cleansed and reserved for men free in body as well as soul. Despite the evils of slavery, it was under this system that the Southern people did a noble work in educating the negro out of African savagery and paganism into the rudiments of Christianity and civilization.

CHAPTER IV.

LIVELY POLITICS IN THE OLD DOMINION.

IN July, 1620, when the Pilgrims in Leyden were getting ready to sail westward, there were four thousand persons in Virginia, and during the year forty thousand pounds of tobacco were shipped to England and Holland. More women came over as brides. A windmill was built. Iron works were established and schools started. Translations of Ovid and Virgil were made by George Sandys and published in 1626. This scholar was treasurer of the colony and brother of that Sir Edwin Sandys, the friend of the Pilgrims and a lover of liberty, who was active in securing a new constitution for the colony, which confirmed and enlarged the powers of government by the people. This famous ordinance furnished the model of every subsequent provincial form of government in the Anglo-American colonies.

Twenty-one vessels came over during the year 1621, bringing thirteen hundred men, women, and children. Though most of the immigrants were English people, yet among them were Scottish, Welsh, Irish, Dutch, Germans, and Poles, and these were followed later by people of other nationalities. The Virginians, like New Yorkers, Yankees, and Western people, are of varied ancestry, though dominated, just as our whole country is, by English ideas, traditions, and language; for the best " English " ideas are an inheritance from the whole Teutonic race.

The phrase " Old Virginia " now came into use, because the Plymouth men made a New Virginia in the North, and later the popular term was " the Old Dominion," an honor which Canada both officially and familiarly, though without the adjective, still enjoys.

The subsequent history of this noble colony was influenced by the fortunes and misfortunes of the English people. Their internal experiences were much like those of other builders of commonwealths along the Atlantic coast. They suffered from Indian wars and from a variety of troubles, climatic, social, economic, and political, both within and without, but the steadiness and great value of the tobacco crop, its easy cultivation and quick returns, made wealth of rapid growth. This single plant, one of the many gifts of the red man to American civilization, gave to Virginia the possibility of being the largest and richest of the thirteen colonies. In the Revolution, Virginia led all in population, having nearly eight hundred thousand inhabitants.

The early representative government was partially

suppressed by the king, who, in 1624, took away
the company's charter and made Virginia a royal
province. Sir William Berkeley, the governor in
1642, did not believe in any education for the
common people, and was an almost fanatical adher-
ent to the political church of England. Nevertheless,
the Assembly was continued and the people made
most of their own laws. When King Charles I.
lost his head and Cromwell and the Commonwealth
arose, many of the Cavaliers left England and emigrated to Virginia. Not a few of these were men
of character, influence, and ability, who became
founders of illustrious families of Virginia and
ancestors of leading American statesmen.

When the Commonwealth was set up, the Virginians gave allegiance to the Protector, and in the
name of this government North Carolina was explored and taken possession of. Under Cromwell's
rule the Virginia people were very prosperous, but
as soon as Charles II. was on the throne again Sir
William Berkeley became governor once more.
Representative government was suppressed in
Virginia, and the royal governor and men of his
mind kept out every sort of religion except that of
which the king approved. Yet although the
Virginians had made a great present of nearly fifty
thousand pounds of tobacco to the new king, and
even celebrated the date of his restoration, May 29,

as a holy day, they found that the second Charles
Stuart was quite ready to destroy the colony if it
were his whim to do so.

Parliament had enacted certain navigation laws,
in the nature of a protective tariff, which were
aimed at the Dutch, then the common carriers of
Europe's trade by water. The idea was to ruin the
commerce of the republic as far as possible, and
thus get the control of the seas. Everything brought
to Great Britain or sent from the colonies, or any
foreign goods purchased, must be carried in English
vessels. In spite of the protest of the governor and
planters of Virginia, King Charles enforced these
laws and even made them more stringent. The
tobacco trade, then amounting to about sixty
million dollars a year, was thus nearly ruined; for
the planters could get only the price which English
merchants chose to give and were compelled to buy
woven stuffs, manufactures, and sugar at whatever
cost was fixed in London. Still worse, the unscrupulous and perfidious king gave away nearly
the whole of Virginia to two of his court favorites,
so that the planters were not only without title to
their lands, but had no votes or representation. The
state of affairs, aggravated by the hostile Indians,
became so distressful that the troubles culminated
in what is known as " Bacon's Rebellion," and civil
war broke out.

Nathaniel Bacon, Jr., who had been but a short time in the colony, was a young lawyer, rich, eloquent, popular, and brave. The people rallied round him, electing a new assembly and making Bacon one of their representatives. The reform measures were called "Bacon's laws." Governor Berkeley resisted, dissolved the council, addressed the king, and proclaimed Bacon a traitor. Bacon marched on Jamestown to the governor's quarters. It is said that he imitated the trick played at the siege of Maastricht by the Spanish soldiers, who bucklered female captives in front of them when they attacked the city. Seizing some of the wives of Berkeley's friends, Bacon placed them in front of his troops, so that the governor's forces would not fire upon the besiegers, and Berkeley evacuated the city. With the "white-apron brigade," Bacon won the victory, and in the morning his forces burned Jamestown to the ground.

Henceforth this site of the first permanent English settlement in America was given up to weeds and wild animals. In 1867, when I visited the ruins, the chief feature seemed to be a chimney, some crumbling walls, and fragments of buildings, but little else to suggest the past. The peninsula has become an island, and under the restoring care of the Virginia chapter of the Daughters of the Revolution, Jamestown has been made a clean and pleasant place for the rambles of the tourist and historical student.

Bacon soon died from disease brought on by exposure. His followers were scattered and twenty-three of them put to death. Berkeley proved himself a butcher, but Bacon the statesman was not forgotten; for many of his laws, though repealed, were reënacted, and Berkeley was recalled by the king. After this, Lord Culpepper was made governor for life and an era of great prosperity began, in which the habits of the planters were marked by personal indulgence and ostentatious expenditure. Virginia hospitality became a proverb.

Though convicts and persons of disreputable character had come into the colony, they were in the minority, and the dangers from this class of people were guarded against by severe laws. The worst met their natural fate in punishment, while the better became prosperous and made good citizens; so that in time a society distinguished for its refinement, executive ability, and generous hospitality grew up in the "ancient dominion." The Cavalier theory of life is not that of the Puritan. The latter excels in self-reliance, endurance, courage, and perseverance; the latter in love, charity, gratitude, and friendship. The Puritan cared little for the graces and decorations of life, but the Cavalier cultivated these with care. There were virtues

and vices among each, and neither lived up fully to
his ideals. A description of one by the other was
usually a caricature. In the old country these two
sorts of men were not able to live peaceably together, until after their civil war and the folly of the
Stuart kings. It seems to have been only through
God's mercy that they were not consumed one of
the other in America. Happily, between Puritan
New England and Cavalier Virginia, Divine Providence placed the tolerant Dutchmen and Quakers.

Though always strongly royalist in sentiment,
Virginia was later powerfully modified in spirit and
procedure by a tremendous infusion of Scottish,
Irish, German, and Swiss elements. These brought
in more democratic ideas, preferring a form of life
less infected with the semi-feudal and state-church
notions of the great planters, which had been imported from Europe. One hundred years after
Bacon's laws had been first enacted, the resolution
in the Continental Congress to declare the colonies
free and independent states came from Virginia.
The decided difference between aristocracy and
democracy, the eastern and the western portions,
tide-water and mountainous Virginia, led in 1861
to the creation of the new state of West Virginia.

CHAPTER V.

WE must now look to that little country on the east side of the North Sea which, after England, has had more to do with the making of our nation and the shaping of American political history than any other.

Holland and Friesland formed part of the ancient home of the nations that helped to form the very much mixed English people. Here in ancient times dwelt the Angles, Saxons, Frisians, and other tribes who crossed over into Great Britain. Later from the Netherlands came most of the skilled artisans, inventors, and financiers, who changed England from an agricultural and wool-raising country to one leading the world in commerce and manufactures. It was the federal union of the seven states of the Dutch republic, with their written constitution and history much like our own, that, even more than England, gave the United States of America their political precedents. Instead of there being a single state made up of many countries, and governed by a king, like England, there were many states, each one having its own government, laws, and customs, though the people all spoke one language. These Dutch states, at first separate, united together, and in July, 1581, declared themselves independent, for much the same reasons as those which impelled the American colonies to imitate their example.

The Dutch believed in "no taxation without consent," and in worshipping God as it suited them, without any dictation from kings or nobles, or church lords. They were perfectly willing to pay for good government, and cheerfully bore the heaviest taxes during their eighty years' war for freedom from Spain, but they believed that those who were to pay the taxes ought first to vote them. Kings, they thought, were servants, not masters. Their flag was red, white, and blue, one stripe for each of the states. Their Congress consisted of a house of deputies, in which the nobles and the cities were represented, and each state had one vote. This body, which represented the states in particular, was called a States-General. As in the case of the United States Senate, which was so largely modelled on the Dutch original, the members were changed every two years. The national capital, The Hague, like the District of Columbia which is copied from it, had no vote.

Their long war of eighty years for independence, begun in 1568 by the invasion of the Spanish army under the Duke of Alva, was the training school of all the English soldiers who were the military directors of the colonies in America. The list is a very long one. It includes Sir Walter Raleigh, Captain John Smith, Argall, and Wingfield of Virginia; Myles Standish, Governor Dudley, and others of Massachusetts; Lyon Gardiner and John Mason of Connecticut; Peter Stuyvesant and Jacob Leisler of New York; many noted Indian fighters and colonial heroes, besides several hundreds, possibly thousands, of men who as veteran private soldiers or non-commissioned officers emigrated to the various colonies. The Dutch model republican army, under the stadholder Maurice, was the wonder of Europe. The rules which governed it, when adopted by Governor Dale in Virginia, made colonization there a success. The Dutch United States set the example of religious tolerance to the American republic. Holland was the shelter land for the persecuted Jews, the Huguenots, the Walloons or French-speaking Netherlanders, and the oppressed of every land. This was long before the " Pilgrim Fathers " arrived in Leyden. There was no absolute liberty anywhere in Europe in the early seventeenth century, but there was more freedom in the Dutch republic than anywhere else. Besides the city charters and written constitutions, the press was free, as it was not in England.

There were Dutch free schools, sustained by public taxation, democratic rule in the church, and popular power in the state. Here we must look to find the origin of many things which are distinctively American, besides of much of what is best in all the English-speaking countries. Here, not only the first English Bibles, but most of the books and tracts of the free churchmen, were printed. These writings in the interests of religion divorced from politics, and of a church with which politicians could not meddle, helped powerfully to bring about the Commonwealth, the popular British Parliament, and the modern free churches in countries where the speech is English. In a word, the Dutch republic was just the kind of a country well fitted to send out successful colonists and to plant the seed of new states. It has been of the greatest blessing to our country that the founders of Massachusetts, Connecticut, New York, Pennsylvania, Virginia, and possibly those of other states received a good part of their education in the Dutch republic.

After Henry Hudson's discovery of the coast-line of what is now the Middle states and his entrance and exploration of the great river from Sandy Hook to beyond the mouth of the Mohawk, there was a great desire among the Dutch merchants to traffic

with the Indians in New Netherland. Parties of
fur-traders sailed up the river called Mauritius,
named after Maurice, the Dutch stadtholder and
commander of the Union armies. In one family of
refugees from Valenciennes, in 1614, Jean Vigné,
the first white child of New Netherland, was born.
Yet there was no permanent settlement; for during
the Truce or Peace, from 1609 to 1621, no colonies
could be planted. Even when opportunity offered,
there was no special need or desire of colonization;
for Holland and the other six states of the Union
were very prosperous. Everybody had employment,
there was plenty of business, and there seemed no
reason why emigrants should leave the mother
country. The Dutch were not Pilgrims or " Dissenters," nor were they dissatisfied with their government or the state church. Their freedom had
been practically won and their faith was established.

Nevertheless, in anticipation of the end of the
Truce in 1621, the directors of the Netherland
Trading Company prepared to aid any volunteers
who would settle the new Dutch province. These
were not lacking; for there were Walloon before
there were English " Pilgrim Fathers." When the
Spanish Duke of Alva in 1567 invaded that part of
Netherlands which is now Belgium, tens of thousands of Walloons, or French-speaking people of
the Reformed Church, fled for refuge into Holland.

Many of them lived in the same city of Leyden
where long afterwards the future founders of Massachusetts found a home. With the Walloons, or
Belgian Protestants, were many Huguenots. One
of these, Jesse de Forest, as early as 1617 came
from Hainault. He proposed to go out under any
protection he could get and settle the new country
discovered by Hudson, from which the fur-traders
were sending home so many wonderful things, but
the Dutch government could not then aid them.

Meanwhile in 1619, Rev. John Robinson, pastor
of the Pilgrims, who formed one of the two British
congregations in Leyden, made application to go to
New Netherland. The directors of the company
were pleased with the idea; for these English folks
had a first-rate reputation. They offered to give
Robinson's people free passage and cattle. They
also asked the Congress at The Hague for two
Dutch men-of-war to protect the colonists against
the Spaniards and King James, but for many good
political reasons the request had to be denied. The
war with Spain was to reopen the very next year,
and the Dutch statesmen could not spare a single
ship or cannon, neither did they wish to offend their
British ally, James.

De Forest then made application in 1621 to the
English ambassador, Sir Dudley Carleton, offering
to take out fifty or sixty Walloon families. The

document is a very curious one, with the contract or covenant of the petitioners in the centre and their names written as in a " round robin," like the spokes of a wheel. England's sovereign gave permission for this party of three hundred souls to settle in Virginia; but, as he was dreadfully poor, and was trying to get along without his Parliament, James could not and would not pay their expenses.

At last Jesse de Forest's opportunity came, when the West India Company was formed. The directors took up his scheme and carried it out in the settlements which became New York, Brooklyn, and Albany. One of the best and largest vessels of the time, named the *New Netherland*, was fitted out. She was of a hundred tons' greater capacity than the *Mayflower*, and three times larger than Hudson's ship of discovery, the *Half-Moon*. Captain C. J. May was made governor of the new Dutch provinces, which included the territory out of which the four Middle states, New York, New Jersey, Pennsylvania, and Delaware, have been formed. Of the sixty families, some were to go to the South or Delaware River, some were to be left on Manhattan Island or the lower Hudson, and some were to be established with a fort at the head of navigation in the Mauritius or Hudson River near the mouth of the Mohawk.

The splendid new vessel sailed out in March,

1623, gay with the red and white striped flag of the Dutch United States navy and of the corporation. This latter was made by marking on the red, white, and blue flag of the republic a monogram consisting of a large *W*, on the right and left lines of which were the letters *G* and *C*, which stood for the Chartered West India Company. Amid cheers and huzzas, with signs of sorrow as well as of joy, the good ship moved from her moorings near the Weeper's Tower, in which the harbor-master of Amsterdam still has his office. On board the clean and comfortable ship were intelligent, God-fearing people, who loved their Bibles and enjoyed worship. Although they had not their pastor on board, there were church officers called comforters of the sick. Four young couples on board were married at sea. The ship after a pleasant passage reached the Hudson River in May.

Inside of Sandy Hook in the Bay, Captain May found a French vessel which had come also to establish a colony, on the basis of Verrazano's discovery of a century before; but the Dutch gave notice that this was their country and they were going to hold it against all comers. Just at that time the little armed yacht *Mackerel* came down the river from Fort Nassau. The French, taking the hint, left, accompanied by their uninvited convoy out into the ocean. Going into the Delaware River, the French were warned off in like manner by the Dutch traders there.

The Walloons were delighted with the new land, which they first beheld robed in the lovely garb of springtime. " Here we found," they wrote back in August, " beautiful rivers, bubbling fountains flowing down into the valleys, basins of running waters in the flat-lands; agreeable fruits in the woods, such as strawberries, walnuts, and wild grapes. The woods abound with venison. There is considerable fish in the rivers; good tillage land."

In the distribution of the colonists, eight men were left on Manhattan Island and some families at the Wallabout or the Walloon's Bend, on Long Island. When this great ship, one of the very largest perhaps that had thus far come to America, tried to go up the Hudson River, her captain found that there was not water deep enough for ships of this class. So when at Esopus Creek, where is now the city of Kingston, he lightened his vessel by putting some of the cargo in boats. The *New Netherland* was thus enabled to make her way up to Fort Nassau, where Albany now stands. There the colonists were landed and began so promptly to plough and sow the ground, probably on the old maize lands of the Indians, that before Captain May started homeward the sprouts were well up out of the soil.

There was nothing slow about the Dutch, despite the sneers we have inherited from our English fathers; for, meanwhile, the military men had laid out a well-built fort, quadrangular in shape, and another fort within a short distance. Eighteen families were left at Fort Orange. Thus began a settlement which in time became the first city north of Manhattan Island, in the whole United States; that is, a settlement having a complete municipal organization and charter. On the Delaware River, Captain May built a fort by the little stream called Timmer's Kill, where Gloucester, New Jersey, now stands. Here eight men were left, besides the four couples that had been married on the *New Netherland* while at sea. It is believed that a fort was also built on the Fresh or Connecticut River, at which two families and six men were left.

The infant settlements were not left alone. In June, 1623, three ships, named the *Orange Tree*, the *Eagle*, and the *Love*, were sent out with reinforcements by the West India Company. These were Dutch people from various states of the republic. Jesse de Forest died, possibly of overwork, in 1626, and his widow returned to Holland together with the young medical student Jean de la Montagne, who, on November 27 of the same year, married her daughter Rachel. No Longfellow, Hawthorne, or Boughton has, with pen or pencil, told of this episode of love, as they have of the Walloon maiden

Priscilla and John Alden. Ten years later, Dr. de la Montagne returned to New Netherland with his wife and children.

The Congress was so well pleased with the success of the company that it granted a seal, such as every province, city, town, village, and community in the Netherlands has to this day. Inside of a wreath were the Latin letters for "Seal of New Netherland," set in a circle surmounted by a crown laid between stars. Within a beaded ring was a shield, within which was a string of beads and another shield on which was a beaver, with his ploughshare-like nose, his chisel-like teeth, his shovel-like feet, and his great trowel-like tail. The beaver was to New Netherland what tobacco was to Virginia, — the emblem of wealth, the substitute for and equivalent of money, and the index of a country to be replenished and subdued. Later the same persevering, industrious, and fur-bearing animal was figured on the first promises to pay, or the Continental money issued by the thirteen United colonies.

The seal of the city of New Amsterdam, on Manhattan Island, consisted of a triple-leaved wreath, with a Latin motto meaning the "Seal of Amsterdam in New Netherland," over which rose the arms of the old city on the Amstel, surmounted by the figure of a beaver. Above this, filling the whole upper part of the seal, was the monogram of the West India Company, laid on an embossed scroll with drapery on either side: When, finally, the seal of the city of New York was made, the beaver, the windmill, and the flour barrel took their places to stay, and still remain. Ignorant people, who do not know the early history of New Netherland, imagine these vessels made by the cooper to have been beer barrels. Englishmen in the seventeenth century probably drank more beer than Dutch, with whom beer has never been especially popular, though it is much enjoyed by Germans.

Thus began, under the red, white, and blue flag, the settlement of the Empire and Keystone states, of New Jersey and Delaware, by industrious, religious, sober people of excellent traits and character. These Walloon Pilgrims from the land of freedom and of heroic and noble stock were soon followed by hundreds of Dutchmen, who came not only from Holland, but from Zealand, Friesland, Drenthe, and from many places in the Dutch United States. In the course of a generation or two, French was dropped and most of the people in New Netherland spoke the rich and vigorous language of Holland.

The republican Dutchmen, although they had still to fight the Spaniards and make their freedom sure, took pride in their North American province. As early as 1625 the Elseviers, the famous printers of Leyden, who very probably gave employment to several of the printers in the Pilgrim company, published a book by De Laet, a director in the West India Company, entitled "New World, or the Description of the West Indies," which tells about the Dutch discoveries, explorations, and colonies.

When Captain May's term of office expired, Verhulst was sent over as governor. Brick trading houses were built. A fresh instalment of one hundred head of cattle arrived. The three ships, containing also forty-five new colonists, were in the convoy of an armed yacht sent by the government. The great neatness and cleanliness, for which the Hollanders are noted, was shown in their ocean transportation of cattle. Such was their skill and care that only two animals died on the passage. Nevertheless, as soon as the poor creatures landed, despite every care, since cows are not botanists, they ate some poisonous weed while grazing, and about twenty of them died. The others multiplied, and soon milk, cream, butter, cheese, beef, and nourishing food were abundant.

By the year 1625, the company, having got all of the capital necessary and the colony being in such a flourishing condition, Peter Minuit, a Walloon, was appointed director-general. Sailing in the *Sea-Mew*, with a proper staff of officers, he arrived on Manhattan Island in May, 1626. His first official act was that of an honorable Christian gentleman, and one that shows the honesty and liberal policy of the Dutch, his masters, who acknowledged the right of the Indians to the soil on which they dwelt. With all due ceremony and form, under the red, white, and blue flag, the governor purchased from the Indians the island of Manhattan, for which he paid them sixty guilders, or twenty-four dollars, which would mean about one hundred dollars of the present value. As the Indians knew nothing, and cared nothing, about stamped metal money in gold and silver, Minuit paid them in red cloth, brass buttons, and various other things, thus getting about twenty-two thousand acres for what seems to us a trifle.

It was not a mere whim of Minuit, thus to pay the Indians for their land; for the Dutch government peremptorily ordered all Dutch settlers to take no land from the aborigines without fully satisfying their claims. From the first, the Dutch policy with the Indians, as men worthy of trust and kindness, was a noble one. New York and Pennsylvania excel all the states in the number of their Indian deeds and tokens of the purchase of land by white men from red. The aborigines were treated with Christian consideration, rather than as Canaanites to be exterminated.

Director-general Minuit found, in the settlement

on Manhattan Island, a well-laid-out fort,—for the
Dutch were among the best engineers in Europe—
a stone trading house, and a few dwellings built of
logs. His council consisted of five members, who
had the power of giving advice and trying offences,
but no life could be taken without reference to the
home government. Besides the councillors were the
secretary and a schout. The first secretary was
Isaac de Rasieres, who had come in the ship *Arms
of Amsterdam.* The schout, John Banope, was the
first sheriff, and combined also the duties of prose-
cuting officer; or, as we should now say, district
attorney, for this peculiarly American office was introduced first in New York by the Dutch.

The first ship returning to Amsterdam brought
good news from New Netherland. The deputy
from Congress, who was present at the meeting of
the West India Company, wrote: " Our people there
[in America] are of good courage and live peaceably. Their women also have borne children there,
they have bought the island Manhattes from the
wild men for the value of sixty guilders. . . . They
sowed all their grain in the middle of May, and
harvested it in the middle of August." He then
gives a list of samples of summer grain, such as
wheat, rye, barley, oats, buckwheat, canary seed,
beans, and flax. The cargo of the ship *Arms of
Amsterdam* contained 7246 beaver, 853 otter, and

151 skins of minks, lynxes, muskrats, and other animals, with much timber of oak and walnut wood.

The government of Minuit seems to have been one of steady colonial development. He left his office in 1633, and was succeeded by Governor Wouter Van Twiller, who served five years. William Kieft was next in office, from 1638 to 1647. Governor Petrus Stuyvesant, the last Dutch governor, served the longest term,—from 1647 to 1664.

CHAPTER VI.

OUR DUTCH FOREFATHERS.

WHAT were the characteristics of the people who first, before 1664, settled the Middle states? What kind of men and women did the Dutch republic produce? What sort of colonists did they make? What did they bring over from Holland, which has entered into our American social and national life? While the Pilgrims have been glorified and the Puritans transfigured, the Dutch have been caricatured by Washington Irving, and Americans have inherited the prejudices of Englishmen. Let history give the facts.

The government of New Netherland was entrusted to a trading company, and the Dutch people under its rule were not as the Walloons or Pilgrims. They had not come, as in Virginia, for either adventure or gold; or, as in Massachusetts, on account of religious persecution; or, as in other colonies, in the name of politics, religion, or philanthropy. They went out of a republic, simply as in later times; the people from the United States, east of the Alleghanies, crossed the mountains and prairies to settle the Western states, that is, to better their conditions, to find new homes in a new country. They had only feelings of gratitude to the land and people in the old home.

Religion and education were cared for in New Netherland. Although the people had their Bibles and catechisms and church officers called "comforters of the sick," they were without a minister of the gospel, until 1628. Then the Rev. Jonas Michaelius, who had been a student in Leyden, while the Pilgrims lived there, arrived. He found that there were in all New Netherland about three hundred colonists. The farmers of Manhattan Island were in great need of laborers. Plenty of timber had been cut and a windmill built to saw the logs into boards. A grist-mill to turn the grain into flour was worked by horse power. Experiments in baking brick from the clay, making lime from oyster shells, potash from wood ashes, and salt by evaporating sea water, showed that the lively and inventive Netherlanders were, like the busy bee, "improving every hour." Some seemed over-venturous. Wood-cutters were in the forest shaping beams, posts, knees, and spars for a great ship which was to be larger than anything yet built, even in Holland, and which was between eight and twelve hundred tons' burden. Troubles between the Indians had begun, for the Mohicans and Iroquois were at war, which spoiled for a time the fur trade. Minuit ordered some of the people from Fort Orange to come down to Manhattan for safety.

A Dutchman calls his pastor " Domine." Scottish folks call a "stickit minister," or a schoolmaster, a " Dominie." The Dutch used good unaltered Latin. We ought to do likewise. In the primitive settlement of log cabin and bark huts, Domine Michaelius organized a church. Although the people were all free, and some rough and loose, like most colonists and frontiersmen, yet the Domine found that many had brought their certificates of church membership with them. Director Minuit and the storekeeper of the company were made church officers. The former gentleman had been a deacon in the Dutch church and the latter an elder in the French church at Wesel, where many English refugees during Bloody Mary's rule dwelt and where the first synod of the Reformed churches in the Netherlands had been held. At the first celebration of the Lord's Supper, in the meeting-house, which was in the second story of the horse mill, no fewer than fifty communicants enjoyed this Christian privilege. Fortunately Michaelius could preach in two languages. He thus served both the Walloon and Huguenot people and the Dutch folks.

The Consistory, as the governing body of a Dutch or Reformed church is called, whether in

Holland, America, or South Africa, consisted of four persons, including the Domine and elder Sebastian Crol, who was in command at Fort Orange. This pioneer was not only a good and intelligent leader, but is the traditional inventor of the "cruller," of which the doughnut is the coarser expression. In the long winter months, when it was difficult to procure meat, Sebastian Crol, whose name was pronounced Crull, made the cruller a pretty fair substitute for steaks, chops, and sausages.

The Domine's letter dated August 11, 1828, and unearthed in 1858, was addressed to his friend Domine Smout of Amsterdam, — that hot and intolerant enemy of the Arminians who was deservedly lampooned by the poet Vondel.

Michaelius wrote about the Indians in pretty much the same spirit as Edward Winslow of Massachusetts did about Massasoit and his followers. The modern science of comparative religion, initiated by the Dutch, who first introduced Oriental studies in Europe, had not then been formulated. At first the Domine thought these men, cased in a skin tinted like old copper, were strangers to all decency, uncivil and unscrupulous, "who serve nobody but the devil." Nevertheless, he at once began to take thought for their salvation, and make plans which his successors enlarged and carried out.

Of all the colonists who came to America, none, in the long run, treated the Indians more Christianly and humanely than the Dutch.

The company promised to maintain preachers, schoolmasters, and comforters of the sick, but they did not at first carry out their agreements very well. Soulless corporations, as a rule, care more to make money than to keep promises. Nevertheless, there were soon in New Netherland four well-educated ministers, learned men and graduates of universities. The Dutch, who founded and endowed the four universities of Leyden, Franeker, Groningen, and Utrecht, during their war of independence, and two more, Harderwijk and Amsterdam, when they had won their freedom, insisted upon a learned ministry. They were more afraid of ignorance than they were of the Spaniards. During the era of their "Golden Lion," in the seventeenth century, the little republic in size, less than half the size of South Carolina, led all Europe in learning and inventions.

Churches, nearly every one of which had a school attached to it, sprang up in the Hudson and Mohawk valleys and on Long Island. Before 1664 thirteen ministers had been provided, of whom seven were serving as pastors at the time of the English conquest, and eleven churches were in existence, besides one or two out stations.

Some of these scholarly clergymen were writers of books, including excellent descriptions of the new country, and some composed poetry. Domine Steendam's verses, "The Complaint of New Amsterdam to her Mother" and "The Praise of New Netherland," are well known.

The Rev. Johannes Van Mechlin was another scholarly minister. He was son of a Walloon pastor at Egmont-on-the-Sea in North Holland. He is best known as "Domine Megapolensis," for, like most learned men in those days, he Latinized his name. He made friends with the Jesuit Fathers, Jogues, Bressanni, and La Moyne. He arrived in 1642, with a party of immigrants, to help build up the patroon's settlement at Rensselaerwyk (now Albany). He studied the language of the Mohawk Indians, preaching and teaching them gospel truths, three years before John Eliot began his ministry. At first the red men laughed, scoffed, or got tired and slunk away, but soon he moved their hearts. From that time, for a century on, Indian converts were common in the Dutch valley churches, besides schools for the religious instruction of the Indian children. In his later days, when at New Amsterdam, the Domine became rather Puritanical and showed an intolerant spirit toward the Lutherans and Independents. This was entirely opposed to the Dutch idea that "where persecution begins,

Christianity ends." By the very next mail from
the mother country, both the parson and the governor were rebuked for their hot-headed folly, and
warned not to be too precise in matters indifferent.
They gave Stuyvesant to understand that in affairs
of conscience all colonists, from whatever country or
whatever church, were to enjoy the same freedom as
in the mother country.

Despite the angry quarrels between individual
hot-headed Calvinists and Arminians, toleration was
the law of the Dutch republic. As early as 1577,
before Roger Williams was born, William the Silent
had laid the corner stone of the Dutch, as it is of the
American, republic in these words: "We declare
that you have no right to interfere with the conscience of any one." Hence it was that among the
Dutch in America, those driven out of New England found refuge in New Netherland. The church
records show that despite some irregularities in
morals, natural to a frontier and colonial life, the
standard of social morality in New Netherland was
not exceeded, if it was equalled, by any colony on
the Atlantic coast.

Other books were written. One was by the lawyer Van der Donck, the "yonkheer," or young
master, after whom Yonkers is named. The literary
activity of New Netherland was very creditable to
so small a colony, for the number of Dutchmen

actually settled between New Castle in Delaware and Schenectady on the Mohawk, and between Montauk Point and the Catskills, probably never at any one time exceeded five thousand. The number of those who came and went, lived or died on the soil, during the forty-one years of the colony's life as a Dutch possession, never exceeded fifteen thousand. On the James River and in Massachusetts, in 1664, these numbers could be multiplied fourfold.

It is hard to get people who are living in prosperity to leave their own homes and to colonize new lands. Emigration from the Old to New Netherland was so slow, that in 1629 the directors of "John Company," as it was popularly called, hit upon a new plan and published a Charter of Privileges and Exemptions. This allowed the directors and some others to be "patroons" of New Netherland. This term is very old in Holland, and means a captain or lord of an estate. Whoever should, within the space of four years, undertake to plant a colony of fifty people over fifteen years of age in New Netherland, should be allowed as his absolute property sixteen miles of territory on one side of any river in New Netherland, or eight miles on both sides, without limit of the land back from the stream; but the land must be bought first from the Indians who lived upon it. The patroon was to own the land. The settlers could only live on it, while even the privileges of hunting and fishing, and the fish, the timber, and the minerals were reserved as his own. Neither the patroons nor their tenantry could engage in the fur trade, for that was to be the privilege of the company. For ten years the patroons and the farmers on their land were to be free from taxes, or service, and were to be protected by the soldiers and sailors of this armed commercial corporation.

Altogether, the patroon system was a curious mixture of great privileges and petty restrictions. Soon after this, two of the directors, Samuel Blommaert and Samuel Bodyn, became patroons and bought lands on the Delaware River. Very probably the name of their settlement, meaning "Swan Valley," had reference to that wonderfully beautiful region along the Waal River in Brabant, where is located the legend of the White Swans which Wagner has made familiar in the opera of "Lohengrin." Kilian Van Rensselaer, an Amsterdam pearl-importer, bought many miles of land north and south of Fort Orange, calling it Rensselaerwyk. Michael Paauw secured lands on the Hudson River which he called Pavonia, which is the Latin for his own Dutch name, which means Peacock.

The Dutch claimed New Netherland by the triple right of discovery, exploration, and occupation. They not only resisted the attempts of the English to enter the Hudson River, but they sent a party of men led by Jacobus Van Curler into the Connecticut River to buy the land from the Indian owners and to erect a trading house there. Since they had first entered this stream, one would hardly have thought it necessary to fortify their title by purchase. Yet to make their claim sure, and to hasten the adjustment of the boundary line between New Netherland and New England, the land for about sixty miles from Long Island Sound, including the site of Hartford, was bought from the Indian occupants, besides another tract at the mouth of the river, called Kieviet's Hoek. The arms of the West India Company were nailed upon a tree to show possession. In the neighborhood of the present Colt's Firearm Factory, in Hartford, where the street names to-day recall Dutch history, a redoubt and dwellings were built and called the House of Good Hope. Here two small cannon were mounted in charge of an old artillery soldier named Hans Janse Eencluys.

These Dutchmen in New Netherland were not the over-fat, beer-swilling, pig-eyed, boasting, and vulgar fellows pictured by Washington Irving. The average Hollander is probably not as heavy in weight as the average Englishman. In his pictures, poems, speeches, novels, and theatres, the modern American and often the educated person makes his

Dutchmen talk German or " Pennsylvania Dutch,"
— which is not Dutch, but late American-German.
The average settler in New Netherland was quite
the equal of the average colonist anywhere from
Maine to Georgia. In devoutness, honesty, social
morality, intelligence, and the enterprise that makes
good homes and supports churches and schools, the
New Netherlander was above the average European
colonist in America.

CHAPTER VII.

THE THREE VAN CURLERS.

VAN RENSSELAER MANOR was the only one that proved an entire success, and this was made so chiefly through the exertions and address of the commissary or superintendent, Arendt Van Curler, cousin of the patroon and one of the noblest characters in all the history of the thirteen colonies. He was a man of sterling character, of generous culture, and of tremendous energy, withal possessed of many Christian graces and virtues. Finding that the only communication with Manhattan Island was very slow, because the sloops were often becalmed in the river, he used canoes and light sailing boats, by which he hurried forward new colonists immediately after their arrival. He imported cattle, swine, and horses, suppressed mutinies, cheered up the people, made friends with the Indians, and rescued or ransomed Christian captives, especially Frenchmen, from torture and death at the hands of the Iroquois. He explored the country round about, and was probably the first white man to make a journey through the Mohawk valley.

In a document still extant he described this fair region in witty and brilliant fashion.

There were three Van Curlers in the colony, and these three were typical of the three distinct types of Dutchmen who settled New Netherland. The least important of them all, Anthony, is the one most popularly known, because Washington Irving has made of him a tremendous caricature. Irving's fanciful sketch has been enlarged during successive generations by comic artists and made into many pictures; while Arendt, who was one of the really great makers of America, is unknown to most people.

Who has not read of the "jolly robustious trumpeter named Anthony Van Corlear, famous for his 'long wind, who led a roystering life, giving dances to the wives and daughters of the Burghers of the Manhattoes," " commandant of windmills and champion of New Amsterdam," who in Connecticut " twanged his trumpet like a very devil," and who at last *Spyt den Duivel* blew his last blast and sank to the bottom in trying to swim the Harlem River, giving his name to Anthony's Nose on the Hudson ?

The historical foundation for Irving's figment of fancy is simply this. A banquet was given to Mynheer de Vries in the angle of the fort, and the trumpeter Anthony Van Curler, or " Corlaer," blew his trumpet at the height of the feast; for this he was scolded by a shopman and a supercargo. This the trumpeter resented, so that for a while there was some danger of a quarrel ending in bloodshed. Anthony the trumpeter having given to each of the mercantile men a drubbing, they ran home, vowing vengeance, and got their swords. However, their wrath evaporated in words. In the morning " they feared the trumpeter more than they sought him." On this tiny pebble of fact, a tremendous superstructure of art, legends, jokes, and caricatures has been built.

Anthony Van Curler's ancestors lived at Stavoren in Friesland, where of old was the rich city and shrine of Stavo, the Frisian Thor whose name we have in Thursday. One of them, a woman, asked her husband, a ship captain, to bring her back "the most precious thing in the world." The good man did so, and returned with wheat. Disappointed and angry, she ordered the grain to be thrown overboard. This was done. The grain sprouted and formed a sand bank, which ruined the harbor, as one knows who has seen the broad grass-grown bar in front of the harbor, called the "Vrouwensand." Anthony came to America in a Portuguese ship and, liking the new country, remained.

The trumpeter was a striking and picturesque figure not only in all the countries of Europe in the sixteenth and the seventeenth centuries, but notably so among those triumphant republicans of the Neth-

"THE TRUMPETER WAS A STRIKING AND PICTURESQUE FIGURE."

erlands who had humbled kings and emperors.
William Bradford tells of the great show and form
made by a richly costumed Dutch trumpeter, who
accompanied Isaac de Rasieres, when the latter
visited the Plymouth men, to bear the greetings of
their fellow-Christians at Manhattan. The republican trumpeters had the red, white, and blue silk
flag hanging from their trumpets. Sometimes this
took on a resplendent phase, as when, after some
great victory over the Spaniards, they used a flag of
twenty-one stripes, or seven series of the red, white,
and blue, indicative of the seven states of the republic. The Dutch were as intensely fond of color
and brilliancy in their art, costumes, gardens, and
heraldry, as they were of plainness and severity in
their churches. Puritans in religion and morals, as
many of them were, they loved all bright and beautiful things and the joys and graces of life.

Jacobus Van Curler, whose name is preserved in
" Corlear's Hook " in the borough of Manhattan, in
Greater New York, was a schoolmaster in New
Amsterdam and a landowner on Long Island. He
stands as a fine type of the educated Dutch gentleman, who had neither poverty nor riches. Governor Kieft, when it was vitally important that the
Dutch and English nations should preserve friendship, sent Jacobus Van Curler into Connecticut to
take command of the House of Good Hope. He

was ordered, at all hazards, to keep the peace. Acting wisely and honorably, Jacobus received the approval of his superiors. He was also one of the ten or more schoolmasters in New Netherland who helped to keep popular intelligence in pace with religion. Afterwards he purchased Long Island from the Indians. Honest, wise, and brave was Jacobus Van Curler, one of the fine types of the middle class among the founders of the Empire State.

It is undoubtedly true that the seaport on Manhattan Island, where, before 1664, no fewer than fourteen languages were spoken, had probably its full share of dram-shops and of the kind of floating population noted for drunkenness, brawls, and immorality. Yet the average life, both at the seaport and the inland settlements, in spite of rough pioneer work and frontier experiences, was softened by high ancestral ideals, ornamented and purified by education, and made beautiful and aspiring by religion.

Arendt Van Curler was among the very noblest of the men who founded New Netherland. He has also one of the best records made by any of the makers of America. He arrived at Fort Orange in 1630. He put new life in the colony of Rensselaerwyk. He quickly showed himself a far-sighted statesman. He understood the situation at once. If the French in Canada were able to win over to

their side the great Confederacy of the Five Nations
of the Iroquois Indians, then they would very likely
get possession of all North America. This Van
Curler determined they should not do. When
Champlain, in 1609, interfered in the quarrels
between the Algonquin and Iroquois Indians, by
taking sides with his arquebus in the battle by the
shore of the lake, he sounded the death-knell of
French power in America. The angered and defeated Iroquois came to Fort Orange, as early as
1612, and supplied themselves with firearms. Eel-
kins, the commander, made with them a league of
peace and friendship, and the Dutch and the Iroquois remained friends for many years. Arendt
Van Curler determined to make this league more
solemn and perpetual. Despite occasional out-
breaks, the policy of the Dutch with the Indians
was from the first peaceful. Van Curler learned
the Indians' language, their manners and customs,
mastered their signs, and divined the meaning of
their secret societies. Before the end of his life, he
was one of the very few white men in America who
knew the most sacred traditions of the red men and
had been initiated into their mystic fraternity. In
presence of their greatest chiefs, at the sacred spot
of Tawasentha, on Norman's Kill, just below
Albany, " the place of many dead," the holy sepul-
chre of the fathers and the seat of Hiawatha's first

civilizing work, he reconfirmed the perpetual league of peace and friendship with the Five Nations of Iroquois Indians.

This was a mighty stroke of policy, which had a profound influence in determining future American history and in saving the continent of North America to the ideas of Germanic instead of Latin civilization. It was like building a great breakwater, or an immovable dike, stretching from the Hudson River to Niagara, which protected the colonies against French invasion from Canada. It was surer, in its intended results, than was the Great Wall of China, which stretches across mountain, river, and plain over a distance as great as between Philadelphia and Kansas City. Masonry and brick could never keep out the Tartars from the Middle Kingdom, but the " Covenant of Corlaer " prevented the French from ever possessing the Hudson valley and its gateway to the ocean. For a hundred and fifty years, the " Bourbonnieres " in the North tried to break this dike of defence, but neither by gold, nor bribes, nor diplomacy, nor by sending their priests among the Iroquois, nor by armed invasions, were the French ever able to win away the friendship of the Iroquois for the Dutch, and the English their heirs. The savages always remained "faithful to the Covenant of Corlaer." This friendship of the mightiest confederacy of

Indians on the continent was most potent in finally deciding the ownership of North America.

When the English conquest of 1664 took place, Arendt Van Curler was at once sought for by Colonel Nichols to have the friendship of the Five Nations transferred to the English. Then Van Curler met the chiefs, and "the silver chain was brightened" and maintained until the Revolution, when the white men themselves, Americans and English, separated. In the long wars in America between England and France, Peter Schuyler and Sir William Johnson continued the work of Van Curler. The Iroquois confederacy was the one decisive element and fact which prevented the French from cutting the chain of the colonies in two by seizing New York and thus dividing New England from the Southern colonies.

The impression made on the Indians by the commanding personality of Arendt Van Curler is easily seen in the title they gave him. The red men addressed the colonial governors, whose names they could not and did not care to remember, in varying terms. They called one a pen, another a rock, or a mountain, or a fish, employing some metaphorical or merely official term, but they always called the governors of New York by the personal name of "Corlaer." To this day, the proud title of Queen Victoria in use among the Canadian red

men is " Kora-Kowa," which means " The Illustrious Van Curler," or "the great Corlaer." Kowa
means great, and Kora is only the corruption of the
name Curler.

Arendt Van Curler was always the friend of order,
morals, and religion. A devout man, a steadfast
friend, a loving husband, yet he was a man of progress. He educated himself out of the semi-feudal-
ism of the patroon system and became intelligently
hostile to monopoly and the selfishness of absentee
proprietorship. He opposed strenuously the selling
of intoxicating liquors to the Indians, persuading
them to use, instead, the white man's beverage, beer,
which at that time, before the days of tea and coffee,
all civilized men drank. Van Curler was one of the
first temperance reformers in America. A man of
unspotted truth, he was believed in even by the
French. He was equally trusted by English, by
Dutch, and by the Indians. He was a man of
impartial justice to all, and, as the greatest man in
northern New Netherland, he was the servant of all.
In a word, he was a man of light and leading.

Arendt Van Curler came over as a young bache-
lor, but when determined to leave the patroon's
service, he led westward a colony of free farmers.
With them he bought land from the Indians of the
Mohawk valley, holding it in fee simple, so as to
give it to children or heirs. He married the widow

of Jonas Bronck, after whom Bronxville takes its
name. This Jonas Bronck, by the way, was one of
the first men in America to own and enjoy Japa-
nese works of art, including one of the splendid
swords for which the artificers of the Mikado's empire are famous. In fiction Mrs. Catherwood has
pictured him in her romance, " The Lady of Fort
St. John."

Van Curler made a voyage to Holland and then
on his return purchased the land of the Great Flat,
in the Mohawk valley. In 1661, with his company
of fourteen men, with their families, he founded
Schenectady, a village fortified with palisades, having the church in the centre. Long considered as
the frontier town of " The Far West," Schenectady
stood against monopolists and men like Andros, for
progress and for free and unshackled commerce.

When Van Curler was invited by Governor
Tracy to visit him in Canada, — for all Frenchmen
were very grateful to him for having ransomed or
rescued several Jesuit missionaries from the Indians, — he started to go. In a great storm on
Lake Champlain, having, as the superstitious natives
imagined, insulted their gods, the founder of the
Dutch peace policy with the Indians was drowned.

How Van Curler met his death was told by his
red friends in a way that curiously illustrates their
geography and religion. In the middle of the lake

lying between the Green and the Adirondack mountains, beside which Champlain fired the shot that gave America to the Germanic peoples, rises a famous island called Rock Regio. This landmark rising out of the water was the ancient boundary between the Algonquin and the Iroquois tribes. A canoe from either north or south passing the shadow of this rock, even in time of peace, except by special treaty, became lawful spoil. Here, as the forest warriors believed, dwelt a god who watched over the covenant and could raise storms and punish intruders and all who displeased him. The Indians never passed Rock Regio without paying homage to the god of the boundary, by casting a pipe, a knife, or some tobacco into the water as a sacred act. Arendt Van Curler laughed at the Indians and their notions, and made comic gestures in mockery. Soon a storm arose, the light canoes were tossed about and overturned, and Van Curler was drowned. This the red men attributed to the anger of the god. They mourned greatly over their good friend.

Arendt Van Curler's name survives and soars through the ages on the " winged words " of the Iroquois language. His memory also lives in " Corlaer's Rock," " Corlaer's Bay," and in " Arendt's Kill," a stream near the city of Catskill; while his city on the Mohawk was long called by the French

" the town of Corlaer " and Lake Champlain " Corlaer's Lake." On the seal of the fair city of Schenectady, which he founded, is engraved a sheaf of
ripe wheat, or what was anciently called corn, for
Curler means Korn-aar or corn-ear. Better than
his female ancestor of Stavoren, did Arendt Van
Curler sow seed, which we still reap in harvests of
national prosperity.

The Dutchmen in New Netherland were determined to have representative government, even
though many of them had settled on the patroons'
manors. The majority of colonists, however, lived
outside of these manors on free land. Under Governor Kieft a representative body was formed for
the purpose of consultation in the enactment of
laws. These " eight men " assembled first on September 15, 1643.

CHAPTER VIII.

THE FREE CHURCHMEN IN EUROPE AND AMERICA.

SWITZERLAND is a little country, not much more than half the size of South Carolina, which has grandly contributed to the making of the United States of America. For centuries her twenty-two cantons, or counties, have been united in federal union. Amid the great monarchies around them, France, Italy, Austria, and Germany, the Swiss have maintained freedom in their Alpine home. Out from their valleys and off their mountain slopes, during the past three hundred years, have come thousands of intelligent people to colonize America. Especially do the Carolinas and Pennsylvania owe much to the Swiss. Many of the ablest military officers in colonial days, and in later times some of our most eminent educators and men of science, were from Switzerland.

Yet the greatest debt of our nation is to the Swiss free churchmen, who separated religion from political control, and the church from the intermeddling of magistrates. These Christians taught and lived and died for the doctrine that lies at the basis of the Constitution of the United States, — that conscience is free. These separatists from the political churches were the spiritual forefathers of millions of American people.

Wherever the Bible is put into the language of the common people and widely read, there will necessarily be great changes of thought, and much intellectual activity. Erasmus of Rotterdam collected many manuscripts, and in 1516 issued a new edition of the Greek New Testament. He then translated the text into elegant Latin, which pleased the scholars, who began to put the Holy Scriptures into the various languages of Europe. In the Swiss republic, the Christian people, through reading the Bible, became convinced that society and the church ought to be thoroughly reformed for the better. They noticed at once the difference between the extravagance and the usurpation of authority by the princes in both Church and State, and the simplicity of Jesus and the primitive church. Such a contrast seemed too great, and as displeasing to God as it was bad for men.

These "Brethren," nicknamed "Anabaptists," were at first persecuted by both Protestants and Catholics. Driven out of Switzerland, they fled to the Netherlands. Soon they and their doctrines had so spread into other countries, that all western

Europe was more or less moved by the new ideas. Some of these Brethren abused their freedom. They became so outrageous in their excesses that no civilized society could tolerate them. But when Menno Simons of Friesland trained and organized, and William, the stadholder of Zealand, shielded and tolerated, these independents in religion, they became a quiet, orderly, and influential people called the Mennonites.

These forerunners of American freedom held to most of the ideas which now belong to enlightened Christianity and the nineteenth century. Yet no one would ever suppose this from the misrepresentations of their enemies in unrevised reference books. They believed not only in the separation of Church and State, in "soul liberty" or freedom of conscience, the abolition of religious persecution, in the right and ability of Christian people to govern themselves, but also in prison reform, in the salvation of infants and of the pious heathen, in home and foreign missionary work, in the removal of the death-penalty for crime, in the abolition of slavery and serfdom, and in the education of women. Menno Simons and William of Orange, as well as Calvin and Luther, are the spiritual ancestors of modern democracy.

It was these free-church Christians who wrought the first reformatory influences among the common people of the Netherlands and Great Britain. Their teachings were actively propagated in England as early as the year 1525. By the year 1550, these had become so widely disseminated among the English people, that it was thought necessary by the government, which was a political and ecclesiastical combination, to appoint a great commission of bishops and others to hunt down the Separatists, and have them tried and burned. European statesmen in that age thought that this was the best way of preserving the church, that is, by the cremation of all nonconformists. Nevertheless, these free churchmen increased, and out of them have grown three or more of the greatest Christian denominations in the United States of America. Other Christians, who have been taught to despise the " Anabaptists," now look upon them as true spiritual ancestors. Slaughtered by the tens of thousands, these fearless thinkers, who honestly tried to put in practice the teachings of the Bible, prepared the way for modern civilization.

In England the reformation came on in three great waves from the Continent. The first movement was propagated by the ultra-democratic free churchmen; the second by the Lutherans, who were led by princes; and the third by the democratic Calvinists. King Henry VIII. made the national church independent of the Roman Pontiff. In the north of England, which was then much poorer and more sparsely settled than in the south, there were reactions in favor of the old forms of religion. In one great uprising, called " The Pilgrimage of Grace," the people, led by discontented nobles, gathered in arms. Mobs entered the churches, flung the Bible out of the windows, set up the cross, and clamored for the old festivals and monasteries. King Henry marched up from the south and put down the rebellion with an iron hand. For months the executioners, with axe, sword, and rope, were kept busy. The horrible sight of corpses on gibbets made both a terror to the mind and an offence to the senses.

Under Bloody Mary the reaction was in the other direction. She put hundreds of people of the Reformed faith to death, while thousands more fled from England to the Continent. In Embden, Frankfort, and Geneva, the Puritan parties were formed and theories elaborated. Yet when these reforming Englishmen came back home, they found that Queen Elizabeth wanted no Puritans, but everything in Church and State uniform. She persecuted both the Puritans and the Roman Catholics. When the people again arose with arms, in the movement called " The Uprising of the North," she crushed this with blood and iron and "covered the whole country with gibbets."

All free churchmen caught in her realm were imprisoned, hanged, or burnt to death.

In Scotland, however, the Puritans won permanent victory. The Bible became the national text-book, the Psalms the Scottish hymn-book, and family worship the rule. Robert Burns' poem " The Cotter's Saturday Night" is the epic of Scotland. The Scottish people are pervaded with democratic ideas, quite different from the aristocratic and semi-feudal spirit which still has possession of English society. What breeds in Americans hatred to the wrong side of England, which has led to two wars and might have led to others, is that also which nonconformists or free churchmen in England also hate and fight. All good and true Americans love and reverence the nobler England, whose good ways and works we are proud to imitate. Next to England, perhaps, America is indebted most for good men and women, in both numbers and quality, to Scotland.

Indirectly the beautiful Mary Queen of Scots had much to do with the gathering of that English company of free churchmen in North England, afterwards known as the Pilgrims, and with their flight to Holland, their crossing the ocean in the *Mayflower*, and the settlement of Massachusetts. We must therefore mention her name first, when we introduce them. Once almost invisible in the world's eye, these Scrooby villagers loom colossal in American history.

When Mary married Bothwell, only three months after her first husband, Lord Darnley, had been killed, the Scottish people rose up in arms against her. She fled into England, to lie in prison eighteen years, and to become the centre of a network of Romish plots. When her son, James VI. of Scotland, was made king, the envoys of France came to Edinburgh to persuade him to enter into an alliance against England. It was then necessary for Queen Elizabeth to prevent such a dangerous union of forces. So in 1583 she sent her trusted counsellor William Davison, an Englishman of Scottish descent, to hinder the alliance and in place of it to form a British league of friendship.

In the England of that day there were no roads, as we understand the term now; for there were then very few wheeled wagons, and even these had no springs. Such things as pleasure carriages were almost unknown, or were brand-new curiosities introduced from the Continent. In the whole country, outside the immediate neighborhood of the few large cities, there were only horse tracks or paths. Four of these, being very long, were called "highroads," — one going south from London to Dover, whence men sailed to France and the Continent; one southwestward to Plymouth, where lay the royal ships;

one westward through Wales, by which one crossed over to Ireland. The Great North Road, longest of all, ran into Scotland. Women rarely travelled so far, and when they did it was on horseback. There were no post-offices or mail-routes for the people, but at certain distances along these royal highroads were relays or inns where the post-riders who carried the government's despatches could get entertainment for man and horse over night. Keepers of these inns were called "posts," who had ready a certain number of horses, in order to help forward the king's business. The later days of stage-coaches, and the still more modern era of excellent common roads and of iron railways, have totally changed not only the methods of travel, but also the face of the country. The work done, in drainage and embankments, since engineering has been elevated into a profession, has converted thousands of acres of deadly miasmatic swamp into fertile fields.

In the time of Elizabeth the keeper of the relay at the little place called Scrooby was named Brewster. He had a bright boy named William, who at that time was a student at Cambridge. The youth was probably home from a vacation when the queen's envoy William Davison came along. As it was in January and probably cold and muddy, it may be that Davison stayed all night and told young Brewster, as they sat around the great hearthstone, before the blazing chimney, of the rich cities of the Netherlands, — then so much more magnificent than those in England, — and of his many adventures in the mighty continental world beyond the little island ruled by Elizabeth. It may be that Davison asked young Brewster how he would like to accompany the queen's envoy and thus see the Continent, should the opportunity come. How can we imagine anything else than that the young student would want to see the world? What youth does not long to travel?

William Brewster did not have to wait long; for only two years later, when the lion-hearted Queen Elizabeth had agreed to help the Dutch in their war of independence against Spain, Davison was sent to the capital of the republic at The Hague. Then young Brewster took his first, but not his last, sea-voyage. Landing at Flushing, he saw this fortified town well garrisoned with Scottish, English, Irish, and Welsh, as well as Dutch troops. He beheld many wonderful sights while abroad, but what he learned was even more important for a man whom Providence was educating to be one of the founders of Massachusetts. The Dutch were then in advance of the world in initiating and working out many things which we associate with America, because we suppose them to have been invented on this side of the Atlantic.

Brewster saw seven states united in a single republic, having a Congress or States-General and a commander-in-chief, who commanded the Union army and who was also governor of several of these states. Printing and the press were free, as they were not in England. Books and papers could be published with wonderful freedom. The poor were cared for far better than in Brewster's own country. Hospitals, orphan asylums, and homes for the aged were very numerous. There was not only a great university with high schools and public common schools, but these were supported by public taxation and in them the poor received instruction free. There was no persecution on account of religion, but Jews, Catholics, Calvinists, Lutherans, and Anabaptists were tolerated and dwelt in peace together. Brewster learned a good deal about federal government. He was also powerfully influenced religiously by his patron, who was a Puritan. Having lived long among the Dutch, Davison had imbibed many of their ideas of religious freedom. He treated young Brewster more as a son than a servant. When the Dutch government handed over the iron keys of the three cautionary towns, Davison transferred them to Brewster, and the young student slept with them under his pillow. Having concluded his business, carrying back to England about half a million dollars' worth of jewellery and silver plate, which the Dutch people had given up as security for the loan of English money, Davison was honored by the Congress with a gold chain, but this he put upon the neck of his page to wear.

Coming back to merry England, Davison was made the queen's Secretary of State. William Brewster spent some time at the Court, seeing the queen and her gay lords and ladies. For a while it looked as if he had a brilliant political future before him and might become a high officer of state, but as his fortune was linked with Davison's, and Davison's with that of Mary Queen of Scots, Brewster's political career soon ended. Under the discipline of Providence he became a Separatist, a Pilgrim, and one of the makers of America. When this unfortunate captive lady was executed by the queen's own orders, Elizabeth contrived to throw the blame upon Davison. His fortunes fell, and he found himself a prisoner and impoverished. In 1590 young William Brewster gave up all his dreams of court life and returned to Scrooby. Had the beautiful Scottish queen lived, or died long afterward in her bed, the story of New England might have been different.

In his new home, his father being ill, Brewster carried on the duties of innkeeper and relay agent.

On his father's death, in 1603, he was appointed "post." He had great influence in the neighbor-

hood, and succeeded in getting godly Puritan ministers in the pulpits. Soon he had gathered together
those of like mind with himself to form a new
church. Sometimes he would go with them over
to Gainesborough, ten miles to the eastward, and
there hear the kind of sermons which he enjoyed.
A Puritan in morals, Brewster in church polity
held to that doctrine of the Anabaptists or free
churchmen which declared that Church and State
should be kept apart, and that only those persons
should be considered members of Christ's church
and partakers of the communion who lived holy
lives. By the year 1605, Brewster and his companions, among whom was William Bradford, who
lived at Austerfield, a mile or two north in
Yorkshire, invited the Rev. John Robinson, a
Separatist, who had lived among the Dutch
Anabaptists at Norwich, to come and be their
minister.

It could not now long be concealed that these
people, who worshipped frequently in the old
Scrooby manor house, were Separatists, who had
withdrawn from the national or political church.
They were dubbed " Brownists " because Robert
Browne of Norwich first taught in English the doctrines of the " Anabaptists " or free churchmen.
Driven from Norwich, where the Dutch Mennonites were numerous, Browne went to Middelburg

in Zealand, where they swarmed, where they first received toleration from William of Orange, and where printing was free. Browne's books were secretly circulated in England, though men caught selling them were burnt.

CHAPTER IX.

IN THE LAND WHERE CONSCIENCE WAS FREE.

"OUT of the eater came forth meat" was Samson's riddle. It was like the bees making honey in the skeleton of the lion which the young Nazarite had slain, for the Separatists to form their church in the very meeting-house owned by their persecutor, the archbishop of York, who had political powers like a sheriff. The free churchmen make a clear distinction between a church and the edifice in which it meets, the one being made of souls and the other of stone, brick, or wood. In that wainscoted room of the Scrooby manor house, New England began. As some of the worshippers walked many miles to come to Scrooby, Brewster, who rented the grounds and building, often entertained them at his own charge.

At last the bishop's spies and informers ferreted out these "Brownists." Being watched, as Bradford says, "they could not long continue in a peaceable condition, but were hunted and persecuted on every side. Some were taken and locked up in prison, others had their houses beset and watched night and day, and hardly escaped their hands; and the most were fain to fly and leave their houses and habitations and the means of their livelihood."

A few miles to the southwest of Scrooby village is the town of Worksop, where the writer's ancestors, the Eyres, lived, and further down in the same shire is Newark, where one of them, named Gervaise Eyre, commander of the king's castle during the Civil War, was slain. The Eyres and the Nevilles were kinsmen, and it was "Gervaise Nevyle" of Scrooby who was the first of the Separatist company arrested by the bishop's spies and put into jail, on the charge of being a " Brownist."

Bradford's record means that the company of men, women, and children, caring more for liberty of conscience than for comfort or even life, tried to get to the land where they knew that conscience was free. After walking over the muddy roads some miles southwestwardly to Boston in Lincolnshire, they were betrayed by the treacherous English captain, who was to carry them to Holland, and robbed and thrown into jail; but as the Boston magistrates were Puritans, they were soon released. It must have been a hard winter for them while waiting for another opportunity to escape; for the laws, which were very severe against them, as Separatists from the political church, and which had been originally aimed against the Catholics, made it criminal to leave England without official license.

Nevertheless, in the springtime, they engaged a Dutch captain to meet them on the shore between Great Grimsby and Hull. Most of the males walked across the country, but the women and children with a few men took boats at Bawtry and dropped down the Trent. When the Zealander arrived with his ship, the women were seasick, the boats stranded, and the tide low. One boatful of the men had got on board, when down the hill rushed a great company of men on horse and foot with arms enough for a battle. To save himself and ship, the Dutchman hoisted anchor and sails and left, getting into a great storm. For two weeks the poor landsmen were tossed on the sea, while those left on land were haled from one magistrate to another and finally released. At length, all got safely to Amsterdam.

Over a century and a half later, when illiterate English house-painters renovated the faded swinging signs of the wayside inns and, instead of " The League of Seven States," painted " The Leg and Seven Stars," and when the United States and Great Britain were at war, John Paul Jones, a regularly commissioned American naval officer, captured off the coast near the place of the Pilgrims' flight a brigantine named the *Mayflower*.

The Scrooby refugees lived one year in Amsterdam, where there were other English congregations.

They then went to Leyden for greater peace and comfort. In this fair and beautiful city, they were at first quite poor, but they held together in good fellowship. Being faithful and industrious, they were able in 1612 to buy a large lot of ground and build on it twenty-three small houses, and one large one for their minister. Their settlement was in Bell Alley, just across from St. Peter's church. Behind them was the British Presbyterian church. To their right was the French church, out of which came the Walloon Pilgrim Fathers, who settled New Netherland. To their left was the city commandery or garrison house where Miles Standish was probably on duty. The English Separatists lived midway between the Broadway with its City Hall and the Rapenburg canal, by the side of which was the University.

Other people of like ways of thinking came from Great Britain and joined them, so that they soon numbered three hundred. During the years from 1610 to 1620, during which they lived in this "fair and beautiful city of a sweet situation," as Bradford calls it, probably as many as eighty marriages were made between the men and women in the company. Possibly as many as a hundred children were born, who grew up to speak Dutch and to understand and like the ways of the people and country. Very probably some of these children attended the Dutch free public schools. It is likely that every year they took part with the citizens of Leyden in the October Thanksgiving Day, when deliverance from the Spaniards was celebrated. This was done first by worship in the church, and then by eating a good dinner, in which the meal called "hotch-pot"—beef or mutton and vegetables stewed together—was one of the chief attractions. Our "hodge-podge" is only a corruption of the Dutch "hotch-pot." The iron pot, left behind by the Spaniards when forced to retreat by the waters let in from the broken dikes, had been brought into Leyden by a Dutch boy named Gisbert Cornellissen. It was then and is still kept as a precious relic. The Dutch Thanksgiving Day, like ours, began as a festival of good cheer, gratitude, and worship. In time it degenerated into a mere holiday such as our own is fast becoming.

Some of the Pilgrim men became citizens of the municipal republic of Leyden, and thus learned all about federal and republican government. Brewster, whom we remember to have been in the Netherlands before, set up, with the aid of his friend, Brewer, a printing press and printed books and pamphlets which they sent over to Scotland and England, just as Robert Browne had done. Indeed, this was the great hope, ever cherished by Robinson and his associates, that they would be able from Holland, by means of free printing, to spread their principles of Independency in Great Britain. Had they been able to do this, they would probably never have come to America.

King James considered these "Brownist" pamphlets as incendiary documents. He peremptorily ordered his ambassador, Sir Dudley Carleton, at The Hague, to use every effort to get the Pilgrim Press in Choir Alley broken up. By lobbying in the Dutch Congress and manipulating the whole line of national, state, and city authorities, from the councilman to the stadholder, Carleton succeeded. The types were seized, and the printing office closed. This was an awful blow to the whole Pilgrim Company; for they could no longer expect to influence friends in England and thus bring about the better times which they died without seeing, but which we behold to-day.

This failure of their missionary hopes was what first seriously turned the Pilgrim thoughts towards emigration, though Jesse de Forest was their next-door neighbor and they had already known of his plans and American enterprise. If they could not print their books and pamphlets, then they could not do very much toward converting Englishmen to their ideas; so they began to inquire where they could go and help to make a better England. There were other things which disturbed their

peace of mind, and made them long for life elsewhere, with opportunity for spreading abroad their
teachings. Above all other things, the Pilgrims desired to be missionaries and work out their ideas
of church government and Christianity, without
either aid or opposition from the state.

Many of their sons, who liked Holland and what
the Dutch were fighting for, enlisted in the Union
army or navy. Or they went off to voyages,
loving adventure and attracted by the prospect of
gain. Others married Dutch girls and settled
down in the country. Their daughters married
Dutchmen, and so it seemed as though, if they
stayed in Holland, they would soon lose their native
language and be lost among the Dutch people.
Being Puritans and country people, they did not
approve of the free and joyous way in which the
Dutch, who hated the late Jewish notions about
the Sabbath, kept the Lord's Day. Then, too,
the truce with Spain was to be over in 1621, and
they might be involved in the sufferings and hor-
rors of one of the cruellest of wars; for the Spaniards were no better then in the Netherlands in
putting down what they called a rebellion, than
they are in suppressing one in Cuba. So these
free churchmen began to talk seriously, and the
youngsters to dream of the romance of American
colonization.

During the peace there was tremendous excitement, both religious and political, in the whole country and especially in Leyden. The Calvinists and the Arminians were quarrelling over theological questions. When these got into politics, they took the form of State Sovereignty as against the supremacy of the Federal Government, and of possible secession *versus* the Union. The two parties named Remonstrants and contra-Remonstrants were then arrayed in deadly enmity against each other. The Pilgrims were stanch Calvinists and Union men, but the great excitements through which they passed, not only during the Dutch troubles, but also in the attempts of King James and his ambassador, Sir Dudley Carleton, to destroy them, must have been powerfully educative and given them a tough moral fibre which fitted them to be the nobler builders of a commonwealth. Thus were Brewster, Bradford, Winslow, Carver, Allerton, and others trained in a free republic.

As we have seen, the first application of the Leyden Company was made to the New Netherland Trading Company, but before the answer of the National Government denying two ships of war for a convoy, offers had come from the Virginia Company in England. One of its members, quite probably Sir Edwin Sandys, brother of Brewster's old landlord at Scrooby, and one of the most liberal of

English statesmen, who opposed the bad king and the Spanish influence, lent the Leyden people three hundred pounds sterling without interest, for three years. This meant to these poor people a sum now equal to ten thousand dollars, in a time when there was not one bank in England, and when the rates of interest were like those in barbarous countries to-day, where men have to pay from thirty to sixty per cent. Later on, the Pilgrims actually borrowed money at "usury"; that is, fifty per cent interest.

It was resolved that the youngest and the strongest of the Leyden congregation should first go to New Netherland and start a colony. If Providence seemed to approve of their undertaking, then the others, including the middle-aged and the old, would come out also, if they could,—that is, if they were not hindered by their intolerant king and the bigoted people in the London Company, who hated "Brownists." How wonderful and exciting must have been the dreams of the Pilgrim lads and lassies from the day of decision!

It was on July 22, 1620, that the pioneer party left Delfshaven on the Maas River, fourteen miles south of Leyden, in the little ship *Speedwell*, reaching Southampton a few days later. There they met the larger vessel, the *Mayflower*, from London. For the first time many of the young folks looked upon old England.

CHAPTER X.

THE Leyden church had sent one or two agents over to England to secure a ship and provisions and make agreement about work for the company, shares, payment, etc. Now they found that matters for the colony had been arranged in a very distasteful way, and besides they had to sell off most of their butter and all their beer in order to pay their debts and clear the harbor. Even then they were poorly equipped. However, the two ships started. The *Speedwell* soon began to leak, and they had to put in at Dartmouth, and again at Plymouth, losing both time and money. After getting well into the Atlantic, the rascally captain of the *Speedwell*, who did not want to cross the ocean, declared she was unseaworthy. So, turning back to Plymouth, the weakest of the company were put on the *Speedwell* and sent back to London, while the strongest and bravest, numbering one hundred and two persons, started on the large ship for a voyage in the stormiest time of the year.

When in mid-ocean the frame of the *Mayflower*

was so strained by the chopping waves and the terrible winds, that one of the great supporting beams of the ship was drawn out of place. Then it seemed as though the vessel would go to pieces. Fortunately, one of the passengers had a piece of Dutch hardware on board, which had been invented some years before. This was called a domme-kratcht, or, as we say, a "jack screw." By this, the stout beam was forced into place, and being held by an iron band and supported by a post, the ship was made safe again. Then they calked the seams and tried to keep dry and comfortable; but shut up in the foul air by the horrible weather, and then after-wards much exposed to the raw winds and cold, it is not surprising that the seeds of quick consumption were planted in their constitutions.

Expecting first to see Sandy Hook and to disem-bark near the Hudson River, the Pilgrims made land-fall at Cape Cod. Instead of a lovely land robed in the verdure and flowers of late summer or early autumn, they beheld leafless trees through which the chill winds of November roared and whistled, with pines and cedars.

Yet pilot Coppin, who had been once across the Atlantic, had not made a mistake in his original reckoning, but something had carried the *Mayflower* too far north, just as it had done Verrazano many years before. What was the mystery? Coppin, and many who like him mistook their course, could not then tell. Foolish people long afterward, with that shameful prejudice against the Dutch which so many Americans have inherited from Englishmen and their wars, like to think that the pilot of the *Mayflower* was " bribed by the Dutch."

The truth is, that men did not know anything then about the Gulf Stream, which probably never was understood until after the time of Benjamin Franklin, who was the first to study it philosophically. This great blue stream of warm water flowing northward had disturbed Verrazano's, as it did Coppin's, calculations. The captain of the *Mayflower* tried to sail southward around Cape Cod, but could not get the *Mayflower* through the rough waters, shoals, and quicksands. Thankful to escape shipwreck, the Pilgrims gladly turned back and the *Mayflower* found anchorage off the point where Provincetown now lies. Here, in the summer of 1897, was unveiled a monument in honor of this historic ship and her heroic passengers.

It was a mixed company on board the *Mayflower*. In the first place, there were rough sailors; some of them were very profane and heartless. The captain and mates did not care to remain one day longer than necessary on this side of the Atlantic, and they gave their passengers hints that they must soon get ashore. Then, the colonists had expected to settle

in New Netherland or within the limits claimed by
the London Virginia Company, but had been compelled by the Gulf Stream, or by Providence, to
settle in these northern regions of the Plymouth
Company, for which they had no patent. They
were, therefore, without any authority or means of
government. Some of the uncertain characters on
board, who were rather free with their tongues, were
already giving out that when on land they were
going to do pretty much as they pleased. Perhaps
the every-day morality of the Pilgrim Company was
a little too severe for them.

It was necessary to agree upon some form of
government. So in the cabin of the little ship the
leaders met together and in the name of God and
as loyal subjects of the superstitious monarch that
hated them, and whom they called the " King of
France," as well as of Great Britain and Ireland,
and even nominated "the defender of the faith,"
they covenanted and combined themselves together
into a civil body politic. They promised all due
submission and obedience to such laws and offices
as should be enacted. To this document, probably
laid upon the lid of a chest, forty-one names out of
the sixty-five adult passengers then on the ship
were signed. Governor Carver was made head of
the colony. This compact, since copied in bronze
and cut in stone and made the theme of poetry and

oratory, was the natural result of the provisions already made by the company in London.

Several weeks were spent in exploring the country by sending out parties on land and over the waters in the shallop. Among the adventures were the finding of corn, the remains of an old fort, the graves of two Europeans, and many evidences of the Indians, such as deer traps, deserted wigwams, trails, and old maize fields. They had one skirmish with the Indians, in which no one was hurt. One party spent a Sunday on Clark's Island.

One of the first things done was by the women, who went ashore to wash clothes. Men and boys helped them to build fires, with sweet-smelling juniper or cedar wood, and to bring fresh water from a spring on the beach. Thus was begun the great American Monday wash-day.

It was not until the 21st of December, in the stormy weather, that they landed and began their settlement at what Captain John Smith had already named Plymouth. Here were a brook of fresh water, cultivated land, and a fairly good site for a town, with a hill near by for a fort, just as at Leyden. On the shore lay a boulder, one of the very few large stones anywhere in the neighborhood, which had taken a ride on some prehistoric glacier or iceberg and had thus been carried down from regions farther north in Canada. This they made their first wharf or landing-place, the tradition being that Mary Allerton was the first woman who stepped upon it.

The men went daily to and from the ship, in the wet and stormy weather, occasionally remaining several days and nights on land, but every day working hard, putting up log houses and covering them with thatch. As in all new colonies, there were great dangers from fire, for evidently these people were not accustomed to build houses and to make good chimneys; but though the roofs were several times burnt off, the log walls remained unhurt. The settlement at Plymouth was a good deal like that in Leyden, with houses in rows, with one wide street between, and the hill fort, in which they mounted their four little cannon. Their food was rather poor, but they managed to vary it with a few wild ducks and geese. The provisions and stores were landed and put under shelter, late in January, by which time they had roofed the Common House, which was at once filled with the sick and dying. It was not until late in February that their fort was in sufficiently good order to be considered capable of withstanding an attack. No human being of the country visited them, until the middle of March.

By this time contagious consumption had broken out, which quickly carried off whole families and diminished their number nearly one-half; so that

only a few able-bodied men were left. Nevertheless, when the *Mayflower* went away, not one of the
colonists returned in her. Even the ship became a
pest-house; for many of the sailors that were living
in the germ-infested quarters of the late passengers
sickened and died. With such brutal and profane
sailors in a floating coffin, it is no wonder that the
Pilgrims, even if any of them had a longing to run
the risk of imprisonment and death at the hands
of their country's rulers, preferred to trust in God
and stay on the bleak shores of Massachusetts.

The coast of Maine was at this time much resorted to by European fishing vessels, and Boston
harbor and the region of Cape Cod were among the
most frequently visited portions of the American
coast-line. The French and the Dutch, having
made explorations and mapped the country, often
paid visits. English kidnappers and slave-traders
were also frequent and dangerous. They seized the
Indians and sold them as laborers and galley slaves
to Spain. Such acts made the Indians very hostile
to white men. No red men lived near Plymouth,
for a great plague had broken out a few years
before, so that no natives disputed ownership of
the soil. Indeed, both Pilgrims and Puritans, for
the most part, took it for granted that all the land
belonged to King James, and to themselves as
representing him.

It was on the sixteenth day of March, 1621, a few days before the whole company finally came ashore, that the first native American, tall and straight, without moustaches or whiskers, and almost naked, except for a little fringed leather around his waist, suddenly appeared in Leyden street. He held in one hand a bow and in the other two arrows. Opening his mouth, he said " Welcome." This was Samoset, who became the interpreter and friend of the colonists; for he had learned some English when on board Captain Dermer's ship. He was first served with food and drink, greatly enjoying his European refreshments. Then he told his story and the history of the place.

Samoset returned to Plymouth a few days later, with five other tall and sturdy savages partly dressed in deer and panther fur. As Gypsies were the only dark-skinned men the Pilgrims had seen, and Irish hose the only garments for the legs reaching from the ankles to the waist, — for the Pilgrims wore knickerbockers or knee-breeches and stockings, — they thought the Indians looked like Gypsies and wore Irish trousers.

Other visits were from an Indian named Squanto, who had been in London, and from Massasoit and his warriors. These were entertained at Plymouth, and thus friendly relations began. The Indians helped the white men and taught them many useful things, especially in the matter of getting food. These Europeans had probably never seen corn before and did not understand its cultivation. Squanto showed them how to catch the fish called alewives and to plant corn in hills, putting a fish with ·the seed so as to manure the soil, which was sandy and poor. He also gave them an object-lesson by going down to the shore and with his feet pressing out the eels, and in some cases catching fish without hook or net. In various other ways, friendly Indians were very helpful. These emigrants did not know the American climate; for they planted some of their best seeds in the soil in February, because the weather seemed to be warm. In this they were at least two or three months ahead of time.

When autumn was at hand, Governor John Carver was dead, and William Bradford had succeeded. The crops had been gathered. Long accustomed to Thanksgiving days in Leyden, they determined to have one of their own. So Governor Bradford sent out four or five lusty young fellows with their firelocks, and the wild turkey being abundant and game fat, enough birds were shot to furnish the colonists for nearly a week. The Indians, being more expert in shooting and trapping deer, provided the venison. Both natives and new-comers enjoyed several days of sport and feasting, though praise to

God was not forgotten. The white musketeers and the red archers shot at a mark and sat side by side along the boards spread with well-cooked game and savory dishes which the wives and maidens of the Pilgrims provided. Thus was begun what has grown to be our national Thanksgiving Day.

Amid the rigors of the climate, homesickness, rough work and hardships of the new life, and the difficulty of getting enough food, these pioneers failed in flesh and color. The survivors of the original *Mayflower* company must have seemed an emaciated and shabbily dressed lot of people, when the *Anne* and *Little James*, the next ships of the Pilgrim fleet, came in. Indeed, the first two or three years were those of severe struggle against famine, hostile Indians, rattlesnakes, mosquitoes, seventeen-year locusts, and various other troubles. As the years went on, however, the splendid faith, the unfailing courage, and the unremitting industry of these brave men and women had their reward. Harvests improved, more land was won to the plough, cattle were imported, and new colonists joined them.

Between 1620 and 1630 about three hundred emigrants, all told, came to Plymouth, bringing colonists from Holland and from England. Most of these were honest, industrious, sober, and law-abiding people. Nevertheless, the bigoted party among the London Adventurers prevented John Robinson from coming over and in other ways troubled the Plymouth people, because they were Independents in church government. The Adventurers even tried to force ministers of the political church of England upon these free churchmen, but in this they did not succeed. In 1626 the Plymouth leaders bought out the share of the London Company, and in a few years owned all their own habitations and stock. When they learned from the Dutch the art of using wampum or Indian shell-money, trade with the red men mightily improved and they became quite comfortably settled, with a reasonable share of this world's goods.

Their former neighbors in Leyden, the Walloons and Dutch, now living on Manhattan Island, wished to open neighborly communication, and in 1627 sent their secretary, Isaac de Rasieres, to Plymouth. He came, bringing his trumpeter and several companions, besides cloth, sugar, and other things which the Pilgrims wanted and which they paid for in other commodities, including tobacco. Best of all, in this visit they learned the valuable secret of Indian currency, by which they were enabled to open fresh markets at a much greater profit. Those Indians east of the Hudson River and north of Long Island Sound were Algonquins, speaking a different language from the Iroquois. The Five Nations occupying New Netherland were a more highly civilized body of men. These used tokens or pieces of shells drilled, polished, and strung together, for money in tráde and also for the making of historical documents to assist their memory. At first, the eastern Indians, not accustomed to wampum, did not take it up very rapidly, but before long the Pilgrims could not get enough of it. Just as tobacco in Virginia gave settled prosperity, so, from about the time of their use of wampum, the Plymouth men had no further anxiety about food or income.

The greatest of their troubles arose from the presence of various bad characters "shuffled in" among them, as Bradford says. From time to time English kidnappers and slave-traders, treacherous redskins and bad men, like Morton of Merrymount, gave much anxiety to the godly colonists. But Bradford's wisdom and firmness, Standish's alertness and courage, Winslow's diplomacy and skill in dealing with all sorts of men, and John Alden's faithful service made a combination of talents that extricated the colony out of all difficulties and secured a success that impressed the world.

In their history of life in and flight from England, their eleven years' mellowing and tempering in the Dutch republic, and in their demonstration that men from different countries and of various shades of religious belief could live together in peace, Plymouth colony was a type of the United States. In this cosmopolitan company were representatives of at least seven nations,—English, Scottish, Welsh, Irish, French, Walloon, and Dutch,—while among them were rigid Anglicans, stern Puritans, bold radicals like Roger Williams, Roman Catholics like Miles Standish, and men of other beliefs from differing religious communities. Yet the Pilgrims, though lofty in morals, were sweet in temper, tolerant to various faiths, and withal full of common sense. Considering all things, they showed grandly how Christian men could live in harmony when united in great principles.

To most readers the poetic side is also the historic side of Plymouth Plantation. It appears in Longfellow's picture-poem of " The Courtship of Miles Standish," which George H. Boughton has reproduced on his glowing canvases. Happy the Pilgrim fathers and mothers and happy their descendants, that they escaped the caricaturist before tradition had set and history had revealed the full truth concerning all of our forefathers.

CHAPTER XI.

THE GREAT PURITAN EXODUS.

"NOTHING succeeds like success." It is masterful precedents that move men to dare and do. More than anything else it was the fact that the Pilgrims had established Plymouth colony in prosperity, that led a great Puritan migration from England and colonies from Scotland, which settled Maine, New Hampshire, Vermont, Massachusetts, Connecticut, and Rhode Island, with people from the four nations of the United Kingdom of Great Britain and Ireland, among whom also were Dutchmen, Huguenots, Germans, and other nationalities.

In the English home land, the condition of the Puritans was becoming daily more intolerable. James Stuart seemed to be falling into bottomless bigotry and Archbishop Laud, his minion, who was very much the same kind of a fanatic that may be found in Mohammedan countries, was filling the English jails with Christians who would not conform to the political church. The Scottish people seemed able to resist the machinations of King James, who said that he would compel all his subjects to conform or else harry them out of the country. In England the elements were gathering for the great civil war which was to divide England into hostile camps and bring a law-defying monarch to the block. This, however, Charles I. little anticipated when he became king in 1635. Ignoring Parliament and trampling on the constitution, he tried to rule the country with the aid of such creatures as Laud.

Besides political and church troubles, there was also much agricultural and commercial distress. These things conspired to make Englishmen willing to leave their own country, and try their fortunes where the fisheries were so rich, furs so abundant, trade promising, agriculture excellent, gold to be found, and silk possibly to be made. Societies were formed for the purpose of promoting emigration to America. In 1626 Roger Conant and the "Old Planters" began the settlement of Salem. In 1628 another company of Puritans, two hundred or more, led by John Endicott of Dorchester, crossed the ocean, hoping to find rest from persecution. They landed on the north or "Puritan Shore," of Boston Bay, and Salem soon became a thriving place. The old wooden meeting-house of 1634 is still kept in this city, which is now the Mecca of the antiquarian and lover of history, and in which Hawthorne began writing those classic romances of Puritan life, including "The Scarlet Letter" and "The House of the Seven Gables."

These people of the "Bay Colony" did not at first separate from the church of England. They were Puritans of the sternest type, not having the spirit of toleration like the Pilgrims, who had dwelt twelve years in a country where conscience was free. Indeed, Endicott hated the very idea of religious liberty. He cut the cross out of the English flag, because he thought it savored of Romanism.

When Charles I. kept on in his tyrannical course, the whole of the London Company determined to move in a body over the ocean and take themselves, their charter, and their government to America. Thus a great host of emigrants led by John Winthrop, who was appointed governor of Massachusetts, came in a fleet of eleven vessels, on board of which were seven hundred settlers, with horses, cattle, tools, clothes, and other abundant equipment for maintaining a colony. These people were not poor like the Pilgrims. Most of them were wealthy, and many of them highly educated, and of excellent social and intellectual culture. They arrived not in the depth of winter, but in the height of summer, when strawberries were ripe and flowers fragrant and abundant. Everything seemed lovely and well calculated to give cheering first impressions. The ships named the *Talbot*, the *George*, the *Lion's Whelp*, the *Four Sisters*, and the *May-flower* were all large and fine craft, some of three hundred tons' burthen. They were well loaded with supplies of fully made suits of clothing, seeds, grain, wine, fishing nets, and fowling-pieces. Military equipments, such as drums, flags, spears, plenty of powder and shot, were not forgotten; for not a few of these Puritans had been soldiers in the Dutch wars. Among the colonists were skilled farmers, gardeners, men who could make pitch and salt, iron-workers, surgeons, barbers, prospectors for minerals, engineers, and surveyors.

Not liking Salem, Winthrop settled at Charles-town, where at first, on account of the poor water, there was a great deal of sickness, but right across the bay there was an inviting piece of land. This was shaped like a lily, with a long narrow stem going back to the mainland. On this ground were three hills. The Indians named the place Shawmut, which probably means the place near the neck, re-ferring to the peninsula, though some connect its meaning with water. The English called the place Tri-Mountain, which has since become Tremont. They soon erected a beacon on the highest hill to guide the ships coming in the harbor. Hence the name Beacon Hill, and Beacon Street. There was plenty of good fresh water at Shawmut, and an

English hermit named Blackstone lived here, who invited Winthrop and his fellow-Puritans to come over and make the place their home. They did so, and the settlement was soon afterward named Boston, after the old St. Botolph's town on the Witham, in England.

This Puritan emigration, on so large a scale, gave to Massachusetts an advantage which no other of the colonies possessed, or was to possess; that is, the early settlement of a very large number of fairly well-to-do and intelligent people of one race, language, and general way of thinking, within a small space of territory. By this providential concurrence of forces, tremendous and enduring moral and intellectual influences were generated which have borne rich fruit in our nation.

In England, it seemed to some that the country would be depopulated if the rage of emigration continued. Probably as many as twenty thousand English emigrants came over before 1640. In the fifteen years from 1630 to the breaking out of the Civil War in 1645, more people came from Old to New England than afterwards came between 1645 and 1775. Among the highly educated people were between eighty and one hundred clergymen, graduates mostly of Cambridge. Often it happened that those on board the ships lying in the Fleet River, before going out in the Thames, had friends or

kinsmen in the Fleet prison, put there for conscience' sake. At last the government interfered "to
restrain the disorderly transporting of his Majesty's
subjects . . . whose only or principal end is to live
beyond the reach of authority." Next day an order
appeared to stay eight ships then in the Thames,
and their passengers were compelled to disembark.
Among those who started to sail for Massachusetts,
but had to get off ship, was Oliver Cromwell. The
Puritans in America very early in their history became Separatists from the Anglican Establishment.
Largely because of the direct influence of the Pilgrims, they became Independents in religion like
the Plymouth men, but, unlike the latter, they united
Church and State.

There was very little of real democracy in the
Bay Colony, but much of aristocracy; for only church
members had a right to vote. In theory, all public
matters were discussed and voted on in town meeting, that is, a town meeting of the church members,
or Puritans. These Puritans could not tolerate the
men of other ways of thinking, like the Quakers
and the Baptists who came among them, whom
they beat, branded, or hanged. They even dubbed
the Plymouth colonists " Brownists " or " Anabaptists," and looked with more or less contempt upon
them. Both in Holland and America, the Pilgrim
Fathers were better treated by the Dutch than by

the Puritans. Toleration is a virtue which Americans have not learned from England, or from the Puritans of New England. For the origins of the religious liberty which we enjoy, we must look to the Anabaptists, William the Silent, and the Dutch republic.

The concentration of most of the people near the seacoast was partly a necessity and partly for advantage. The soil not being especially fertile, large farms like those in Virginia were unknown. Many of the people had come chiefly for the purpose of fishing. Shipbuilding and commerce soon flourished. The *Blessing of the Bay* was launched in 1630. Quite early in the history of the colony, large fleets, with thousands of men, found employment and wealth in the Newfoundland fisheries. The codfish became a symbol of the new riches, giving its name to the aristocracy whose fathers had drawn treasures out of the sea. A golden codfish hangs to-day, as the emblem of colonial wealth, in the halls of the legislature of Massachusetts, which was then and is still called the General Court.

It was quite common to see shipyards and farms alternating along the seacoast, and even to see shipbuilding going on in front of a farm, between the crops and the blue water. Prepared lumber, in the form of staves for barrels, were sent over to the old country. American-built ships were sold in Europe. Friday food was supplied to the southern nations. When commerce was opened with the West Indies, sugar and molasses were abundantly imported. The frequency of candy stores was early noted, while New England rum, made from the juice of sugar-cane, became a common drink, that was enjoyed by all, from the parson to the day laborers. Too free indulgence in the extract of molasses led to many scandals and furnished the stocks with many a victim. Not a little trade was done in slaves. One of the industries was the making of manacles for the supply of the African man-stealers and traders in human flesh.

The intolerant ideas which the Puritans brought with them and which were common to almost all countries in Europe, except Holland, soon had its legitimate results. The Puritans were not only very rigid in their ideas of possessing the earth so as to expel all intruders who did not agree with them, but they also ignored all claims of the Indians to the soil. They believed their land tenure was from the Almighty, through King James. In 1631 Roger Williams arrived at Nantasket. He was a radical who claimed that no one should be bound to maintain worship against his own consent, and that the land belonged to the Indians and they ought to be paid for it.

These were ideas which lay at the basis of the
Dutch republic and their colony in New Netherland, but such free utterances seemed very dangerous. Fearing that King James might take away
their charter and otherwise molest them, the Massachusetts Bay Colony ordered Williams to leave
the colony. He found refuge for a little while in
Plymouth. There, Bradford and other men of like
spirit greatly enjoyed his preaching, despite his
radical notions, for Roger Williams, take him all
in all, was a very lovely character, a true Christian
with little stiffness or formality in his ways, and of
a winsome character.

Travelling through the snow of winter, Williams
went among the Indians, who welcomed him, while
he learned their language. In the springtime he
reached Narragansett Bay, the region which the
Dutch had already named Rood Eilandt (Red
Island), which has since become Rhode Island.
Five friends joined him and they built a shelter on
the Seekonk River. But the Plymouth men, who
in some respects were as greedy of land as the
Puritans, and respected neither Dutch nor Indian
claims, notified him that the region he had chosen
was under their control and intimated that he must
move on. So, getting into their canoe, these apos-
tles of "soul liberty" dropped down the river and
coming in front of the flat ledge of rock, which is

now at the foot of Powers Street in the city of
Providence, they heard the Indians call out two
words, learned from the English, "What cheer!"
Thus welcomed and led by the first dwellers on the
soil, Williams and his friends found a hill and a
spring of excellent water. There they began a
settlement, named, in gratitude to God, Providence,
which has become the second city of the Eastern
states.

It was not long before others joined Roger Williams; and the colony of Providence soon became a
place very agreeable to those seeking "permission
of differing consciences," for here men were awarded
the same liberty as in the Dutch republic. Protestants of all sorts, Catholics, Jews, Agnostics, and
Secularists were protected, just as in the land behind the dikes. This, the less liberal-minded people on both sides of the Atlantic could so little
understand, that, just as they had called Holland
and Amsterdam all kinds of opprobrious names and
the Pilgrims "Brownists," because of the liberty of
conscience granted, so they dubbed Rhode Island
"The Land of Crooked Sticks." This was because
there were, along with many persons of excellent
character, some odd and strange specimens of human nature. Yet, although Roger Williams is
called the founder of soul liberty, he did nothing
more than expand and put in practice ideas which

"'WHAT CHEER?'"

he had already learned from the people of the republic, with whose history he, like Lord Baltimore,
was well acquainted, and with whose language he,
like William Penn, was so familiar.

The next person to come into contact with colonial intolerance was Mrs. Anne Hutchinson, a pure
woman of much intellectual power. She attacked
especially the formalism and what she thought to
be the hypocrisy of the clergymen, whose stiff and
precise ways she evidently did not like. For such
a character as she, who preached and taught her
ideas very vigorously, there was then no room in
Massachusetts. The General Court, after deciding
that Mrs. Hutchinson was " like Roger Williams or
worse," banished her. With others in sympathy
with her, she left for the south, where, in 1638, with
William Coddington they bought Rhode Island
from the Indians and began the colonies of Portsmouth and Newport, which were later followed by
that of Warwick. This lady, the mother of fifteen
children, left Rhode Island in 1642 and settled in
New Netherland. There she and her family were
slain by the Indians.

Roger Williams was too much of a Christian
to nurse any grudge against his persecutors, and
he gave them a splendid object-lesson in practical Christianity. When the Pequot Indians in
eastern Connecticut not only plotted to destroy the

white men who had settled near them, but also intrigued with the Narragansetts to attack Boston and the surrounding towns, Williams' influence in this tribe was so great that he was able to dissuade them from taking the war-path and thus to save the Bay Colony from grave peril.

By 1644 the colonists had greatly increased in the region of Providence and Newport, and liberal ideas and rulers being then in authority, Williams went to England and secured a charter which gave the people the right to frame a government according to their own ideas, provided they were loyal to the supreme authority in England, under which the united colonies formed a province called Rhode Island. This charter was later confirmed and remained the constitution, even until the year 1842.

Rhode Island, more than any other colony or state, partly because of her small size, but primarily because of her founder, carried out most consistently and steadily the idea of absolute religious freedom. Here in the Western world, the Hebrews first found welcome, peace, and prosperity.

The very flower of English Puritanism having left England and settled in Massachusetts, it was natural that so many people of education, among whom there were hundreds of men who had travelled in the Netherlands, and had seen the free common schools in that country, should be earnest

for popular as well as the higher education. As
early as 1635, it was resolved to establish a public
school in Boston. This was two years later than
the school founded on Manhattan Island, which
is still in existence. In 1836 the General Court
voted four hundred pounds, or what would now
be equal to about four thousand dollars, to found
at Newton, or later Cambridge, what is now Harvard University. When, in 1638, the Rev. John
Harvard left his library and about three thousand
dollars to the college, it was named after him.
To the maintenance of this magnificent institu-
tion — magnificent in its origin, as well as in this
time of world-wide fame — the New England people always contributed their generous support.

Printing presses and type were brought over
from Holland, and books, many of which are now
famous in history, were printed on the college
press. Other private and public libraries, increasing with that of Harvard, have brought together
in eastern Massachusetts the largest collections of
books on this continent. It is no wonder that
about nine-tenths of the writers of American history have done most of their work within a cir-
cuit of ten miles from the Massachusetts State
House, and that American history, as thus far
written and popularly read and believed, is rather
a history of New England, with some notices of

parts adjacent and beyond, than of the whole United States of America, and of the people and forces which united to make our country.

Like that of the Swedish and German nations, the Dutch Calvinists, the Catholics of Maryland, and the Pilgrims of New Plymouth, one great idea of the Puritans in founding Harvard College was to convert the Indians to Christianity. Following the good example of the Lutheran Fabricius in Delaware, and of Domine Megapolensis, the Rev. John Eliot, in Massachusetts, began studying Algonquin, and was soon able to preach in that tongue. He gave his hearers long sermons, which were probably no longer than the harangues of their sachems, but he encouraged them, the braves with tobacco, and the squaws with apples. Eliot even translated the Bible, which few persons now can read; for in the Indian, as in all languages except dead ones, words become obsolete, because human speech is a living growth.

Probably as many as a hundred Indian words have become part of our English tongue. Not only are "tomahawk," "moccasin," "caucus," and "mugwump" familiar to us, but so, also, are many names of famous chiefs and tribes. Our mountains and our rivers still reëcho their sonorous aboriginal Indian names, while most of our local poetic legends and American mythology have descended to us from the red men. We are "debtors not only to the Greeks, but to the barbarians," not only to old and new Europeans, but also to the primitive Americans.

Among the other great gifts of the red men to civilization, which have mightily helped in the development of this continent and the white race, are, their skill in getting food out of the sea and soil, by hand, trap, or craft; their great trails and paths; their methods of agriculture; their articles of vegetable food, such as succotash, pumpkins, and corn; their medicines and remedies, ginseng, various roots and products of the forest; the moccasin, the snowshoe, the birch-bark canoe, — all of them most valuable means of exploration, trade, and communication. The political proced- ure of the Indians must certainly have informed and stimulated our fathers; for the caucus, the confederacy, and other ideas learned from the senators of the forest have become part of our own. The friendship of the Iroquois confederacy, first of five and then of six nations, which rose like a dike, impregnable to all assaults of French craft or force, bribery or subtlety, was one of the great decisive elements for winning this continent to Germanic civilization or, as we like to say, to Anglo-Saxon ideas.

In all their education, however, the Puritans did not easily learn the lesson of tolerance; for the Bay Colony was mostly under the rule of the clergy. Lawyers were next to unknown, and physicians as yet had scarcely any social standing. It was not until the time of Cromwell that even surgeons began to have an official position in the army. When the people called Quakers arose in 1656, it seemed to the Puritans as if the Anabaptists had come to life again. Two Quaker women, on landing in Boston, were at once clapped into jail and their books burnt, while they were sent back by the first returning ship. Nevertheless, days of fasting and prayer that were called failed to bar them out, and the Friends kept on coming. The trouble was, that some of these Quakers were rather violent in their behavior. They seemed to be a little better than anarchists. They would not use the ceremonies of society or uncover their heads before the magistrates, and in those days when pomp and ceremony were considered almost a part of religion, this seemed to be an insult to authority itself. The Friends would not take oath in a court of justice, but literally obeyed the command of Christ as to yea and nay. They would not pay taxes to support the state church, which was Congregational in form, nor would they enter military service or bear arms in their own defence.

William Penn had not one musket among all his Quaker colonists.

As in many controversies to-day, the root of the trouble lay in the question as to the seat of authority. Where was it? In the church, or in the Bible, or in one's own conscience? This question has been settled by the American people so far as to declare that it is not the business of the state to decide; for they who obey the laws of the United States can answer the question as they please.

In those days also, when insanity was not well understood, lunatics, instead of being kindly and carefully treated, with comforts and moral suasion and the application of no more force than was necessary, were served in a way that now seems to us cruel and even brutal. The Quakers who ran naked through the streets, or interrupted the meetings, or loudly called the clergymen hypocrites and deceivers were publicly whipped, put in the stocks, maimed, branded with red-hot irons, had their ears cut off, or were exiled. Finally, four of them were hanged on Boston Common, one of them being a woman. When the king interfered, the punishments and the excitement died out.

In those colonies where abundant freedom was granted, the people had little or no trouble with the Quakers, so called. At Plymouth, the Friends would probably have met with no opposition had they come while the original settlers were still alive. It was noticeable, however, that the second generation of people born in the new and rough lands, who had never known either the manly outdoor sports of Merry England or the noble toleration of Holland, and who were influenced by Puritan notions, were much harsher and severer than their fathers. Even in Plymouth the Quakers were whipped and the man who harbored or defended them was suspected and apt to suffer. Laws were even made denouncing death to the Quakers, but happily they were not enforced. Throughout their history the Pilgrims always set the Puritans a noble example of Christianity, charity, and liberal-mindedness.

CHAPTER XII.

CONNECTICUT, RHODE ISLAND, AND NEW HAMPSHIRE.

NO one can ever accuse the Puritans, or the average Englishman, of a lack of courage. The love of war inherited from their Teutonic and Keltic ancestors, and the power to fight with bull-dog tenacity, still remains. After the sachem Massasoit had died, his younger son Metacom, ridiculously called "King" Philip, formed a league of the savages, and in 1675 suddenly attacked the Massachusetts towns.

A war, lasting two years, broke out, which wiped out thirteen towns and resulted in a loss of life probably amounting to six hundred colonists. During all this crisis, Eliot's Christian Indians remained faithful to the whites. After his tribe had been nearly annihilated, Metacom was shot at Mount Hope, near Bristol, Rhode Island, by a party under Captain Benjamin Church. The chief's head was exposed in true European fashion on the palisades at Plymouth, where in time a pair of wrens made their nest inside the skull.

The Indian prisoners were sold as slaves among

the Spanish possessions of South America and the West Indies. Against this un-Christian policy of revenge, some of the clergymen protested in vain. The annals of the Eastern states are fearfully disfigured by the harsh treatment of Indians by Christians. The policy of Roger Williams, Arendt Van Curler, William Penn, and the Moravians was not the policy of these cultured Puritans, who seemed to be far more familiar with the Old than with the New Testament, and who followed the precepts of Joshua and Gideon rather than those of Christ.

With all their Christianity and their civilization, the settlers of the Eastern states were men who inherited the traits and superstitions which had come down from their Germanic ancestors, and these they brought with them to America. They were led astray by their inbred delusions, just as we have seen the Spaniards were by theirs.

Witchcraft is not the curse of any one age or nation, but exists all over the world to-day, wherever old paganism still holds the human mind in slavery, and it lingers even in countries called civilized. The first voices in modern times against it were raised in the Dutch republic, by men who had critically examined the delusion and the alleged manifestations of it; so that by the time the Pilgrims reached Leyden, it had ceased to trouble the minds of most intelligent people. Educated men in Holland everywhere scouted the idea that the devil, or evil spirits of any kind, had any direct dealings with or influence upon the human body, though some clergymen and their adherents still nursed the horrible superstition which they tried to bolster up by quoting the Bible. In 1690 Rev. Balthazar Bekker wrote the book which helped to destroy forever the curse of witchcraft, by attacking the theological theory on which it was founded. The Pilgrims were entirely free from this superstition, and so also were the Massachusetts people who had settled in the Merrimac valley.

Many tens of thousands of people were put to death in various countries of Europe for the supposed crime of witchcraft. King James was a great witch-persecutor. On his return voyage from Denmark, whither he had gone for his bride, he was kept back by contrary winds. These he imagined were raised by Scotch witches, who had come out to sea in sieves for the purpose of troubling him. This James, the fool-king, wrote a book on witchcraft and published it in Edinburgh, in 1597. He issued a new edition in London in 1603, and had a new and more terrible statute against witches passed, under which fresh persecutions broke out in Great Britain and the New England colonies. The epidemic bred by James' new law began in Connecticut, and before 1652 there were thirty

trials of accused persons and eight capital execu-
tions. Then the delusion quieted down.

Forty years later, the insanity broke out at
Danvers or Salem village, in Massachusetts. There
were no lawyers. Trials were held without any
cross-questioning of the witnesses or the sifting of
evidence, and only intolerant clergy and the royal
governor had oversight of the tribunals. When
some young folks charged that certain old women
tormented them by coming through keyholes and
sticking pins in their flesh, they were believed.
Then the excitement quickly became an epidemic.
Like a virulent and infectious disease, the delusion
ran its frightful course. Certain persons were
charged with being in league with the devil and
his imps, and were sentenced to death. None of
them was burned, as many thoughtless people say,
but nineteen people were hanged.

The place is still called Gallows Hill, on which
this judicial murder was perpetrated. When, a few
years ago, the two-hundredth anniversary of this
sad episode was celebrated, the writer of this book
subscribed one dollar to a citizen in Salem, who had
proposed a monument in honor and vindication of
the victims of the Salem witchcraft, but the money
was returned and nothing has been done.

There are some who think that the panic at
Salem was largely caused by Cotton Mather's writ-

ing " Memorable Providences." It is certain that the Salem people quickly awoke to their senses, and in 1693 all convicted and accused persons were set free. Finally, this nightmare of Christendom was lifted. Common sense and science asserted themselves, and the Bible ceased to be misused in the interests of paganism. On the whole, it is remarkable that in all the English colonies, the witchcraft delusion broke out in so few places, although in England the law in favor of witch-killing was not repealed until the year 1736.

Even John Wesley, however, in 1768 said, " The giving up of witchcraft is in effect giving up of the Bible," which is much like what some people say in our day of the literary or higher criticism of the Scriptures. Holland led off in the reforms, and England followed. After these, Germany, Spain, and Scotland, in their order, were the countries in which the greatest number of victims suffered death. As late as 1873, witches were judicially burned in Mexico.

Only two of the original thirteen colonies took their names from the Indians. These were Massachusetts and Connecticut, the first from a hill, and the second from a river-valley. The coast and some parts inland north of Long Island Sound were first explored by the Dutch, more particularly by Captain Block, whose name remains on Block Island and who gave the name Fresh to the river. Another great stream that furnishes Connecticut with a timber slide and with water power has taken its name from that part of the state which the early Dutch called Woesten Hoek, or the wilderness region or corner where the wild men live. This word, as pronounced by Indians, has become " Housatonic." Claiming this land by virtue of discovery and a part of New Netherland, the Dutch governor, as we have seen, sent a party of men first to carry out the usual policy of buying the land from the Indians, and then to erect the House of Good Hope, near the site of Hartford.

The Plymouth men also claimed this region as lying within their patent; but as both they and the Dutch desired to live together before the savages in peace as Christians, and not to get to fighting among themselves, to the scandal of religion, they refrained from hostilities. It was only late in his lifetime that Governor Bradford, probably under pressure from others, wanted to get the Bay Colony to help them to expel the Dutch. The New Netherlanders had no desire to go to war with their Protestant neighbors. Their home government ordered them, above all things, to keep the peace; for brave little Holland was still fighting mighty Spain for her liberty and needed England's friendship.

The English, however, coveted the trade of the Indians, and longed to occupy these fertile acres in

the river valleys, and Englishmen are rarely ever
known to be too hesitant or delicate about seizing
possession of any part of the world when they want
it. We soon find the Eastern colonists moving into
the Connecticut valley, without much regard to other
claimants of ownership. In 1633 Lieutenant William Holmes, unharmed by the Dutch, sailed up the
river in a vessel having on board the frame of a
house, and soon emigrants from the Bay Colony began the towns of Wethersfield and Windsor. A few
months later the English Company, which possessed
a grant from the king, sent out John Winthrop, a
son of the Boston governor, who built a fort at the
mouth of the Connecticut River. He tore down the
Dutch signs of ownership, and named the fort after
two of the chief stockholders of the company, Lord
Say and Brook, — Saybrook.

When news reached the coast settlements that the
country so near New Netherland had been settled,
the Boston and Plymouth folks spoke of the new
region as " the West." Hearing of its fertile soil,
some of the newcomers, who did not like the rather
severe government of the Massachusetts Colony, resolved to emigrate. It must not be forgotten that
some of these Massachusetts colonists were old soldiers who had served in the Dutch war, or others
who had been in the republic, and who could not
stand the rather close social atmosphere. Among

the latter was Thomas Hooker, a Cambridge graduate, who had been persecuted for his nonconformity in England, and who had lived three years in Delft and Rotterdam. He had come secretly to America, for King Charles was having the emigrant ships searched and even stopped from sailing. Another leader was John Davenport, a Puritan divine, who had been ejected from the political church in England, and afterwards spent two years in Holland. When in New Haven, believing that Charles II. had justly lost his head, he gave shelter to two of the judges, called "regicides," because they had ordered Charles Stuart, the law-breaker, to the block.

Hooker found a company of about one hundred people, young and old, men and women, who were willing to go with him. So they started to "go West," taking a two weeks' walk through the woods, crossing the rivers on rafts and finding their way without any guide, except the compass and the sun and stars. They also drove before them their cattle and hogs, and had the fresh milk of the cows to live upon. In health and safety they joined the little settlement of Englishmen at Hartford. Davenport and his colony came later by water. Landing in 1638, at a spot in New Haven now marked by a tablet, they held divine service under a great oak tree, Davenport preaching a sermon in the open air. In the spring they met in a large barn and agreed upon a form of government.

The Connecticut settlers did not seem to have sufficient tact, or else the love of peace in them was not strong enough, to enable them to live quietly with the Indians. When the Pequots threatened to destroy the white settlers, the men of the three towns in the Connecticut valley, — Hartford, Wethersfield, and Windsor, — instead of punishing the ringleaders, agreed to exterminate the Pequots in their stronghold. For this purpose they raised ninety men and put them under the command of Captain John Mason, a veteran of the Dutch wars. With some friendly Mohicans and Narragansett warriors, — though Roger Williams had persuaded the main tribe not to fight, — Mason attacked and surprised the Indian fort. By sword, bullet, or fire, about five hundred Pequots were destroyed. In another expedition in western Connecticut, Captain Mason nearly annihilated the tribe. Thus the Indians paid the awful penalty of the murders which they had committed.

Those settlers of Connecticut led by men who had seen how a country could be governed without a king, under a written constitution, were quite different from the people in the Bay Colony. The society of Massachusetts was rather aristocratic in form. Royalty had many favorites. Towns, villages, and streets were frequently named in honor of the king or his friends. Indeed, one can almost read in the place and road names of Massachusetts the history of Great Britain's royalty and of the different countries from which the kings came. On the contrary, in Connecticut, the spirit of the people was from the first very democratic. They avoided whatever savored of nobles, courts, and kings. Except Windsor, which was settled by Massachusetts people, one will not find in the whole state the name of any king or his favorites. Two reasons, out of many, for this lie in the Dutch leaven imported by Hooker, Davenport, Mason, and other denizens of the republic, and in the large infusion of Welsh emigrants. Moreover, a considerable proportion of family names in Connecticut despite great changes in form and spelling, are unmistakably of Netherlandish or Huguenot origin.

The first political arrangements of Connecticut were wonderfully like those in the Dutch United States, in which Davenport, Hooker, and Mason, and perhaps other prominent men in Connecticut, had spent some time. These resemblances to things in the republic which sheltered the Pilgrims, and in which all the colonial military men were trained, is more than accidental. In 1639 the people of the three towns met, and, after the model of the Dutch republic, drew up a written constitution. The spirit of Hooker, who preached that authority under God resides with the people, took form in writing. No mention was made in the text of the King of England, or of the company holding the king's grant. Suffrage was not limited to church members, but all citizens were equal in political privilege. In the legislature the basis of representation was not by population, but by towns, each having one vote. After the Frisian fashion, the written ballot was used. The duties of the magistrates were substantially those of the Dutch schepens. The colonial government of Connecticut was the closest of all the colonial types of the later national government of the United States.

Out of the Plymouth Company's territory, which received the name of New England, no fewer than seven colonies were formed. Massachusetts at first and for a long time claimed the territory of Maine and New Hampshire. Maine was governed as part of Massachusetts, not becoming a state until 1820, the people being ruled meanwhile under the Andros charter.

"Maine" is the same word as "main" in mainland. At the Centennial Exposition of 1876, in Philadelphia, a man from Augusta, on inquiring for "the Maine building," was shown the largest on the grounds, — the Main Hall. Thereupon he remarked, "Well, I knew that our boys would do the handsome thing." Some French people believe that, since their countrymen settled the northern portion of this wonderful region of the pointed firs, the name was taken from the Gallic province of the same name. Another name frequent in early history is Laconia, which some think arose from the numerous lakes for which Maine is still famous, or because the territory was supposed to extend to Lake Ontario.

No other state has so beautiful and variegated a rocky coast-line, or so many indentations, giving a water frontage of nearly twenty-five hundred miles, or such abundance of natural water power. Maine excels in the number of bold landmarks, such as rivers, mountains, and sheets of water. Its area is nearly equal to that of all the other Eastern states. Its chief products are ice in winter and granite in summer. The population is probably of purer English stock than any other state, and it is famous for the number of great men which it has produced.

New Hampshire received its name through John Mason, a native of the county of Hampshire, England, who settled on the Piscataqua at Dover, in 1627. Before this time a Scotchman named David Thompson, who has an island in Boston harbor named after him, had made a successful settlement at the same place in 1623, and was in friendly coöperation with the Pilgrims. The Plymouth Company had, as early as 1623, made a grant of the country between the Merrimac and Kennebec rivers to John Mason and Sir Ferdinando Gorges, who had served in the Dutch war. After a few years, these proprietors decided to divide the territory. Mason took the land west of the river, while Gorges took the eastern division. In 1638, when Rev. John Wheelwright was expelled from Massachusetts for sympathy with Mrs. Hutchinson, he and some of his congregation moved northward and settled the town of Exeter.

The scattered population, being constantly exposed to the inroads of the French and hostile Indians, kept by the seashore. The settlements of New Hampshire were mostly fishing villages, among which Portsmouth and Dover were the largest. In 1641 the little colony asked to be united to Massachusetts. Not liking the restriction of the ballot to church members, they were allowed to vote and hold office without question as to their membership in religious societies. In later years Scottish and Irish settlers brought to the colony, which became the Old Granite State, the splendid qualities for which this Scotch-Irish stock is deservedly famous. The New Hampshire colonists always took part generously and bravely in the colonial wars and enterprises. They numbered eighty thousand souls at the opening of the Revolution.

Vermont was first looked upon by a white man when Champlain came down the lake named after himself. It was for ages the battle-field and hunting-ground of the Algonquin and the Iroquois Indians. The former tribes had first possession of it; for almost all the Indian names of lakes, rivers, and other landmarks are Algonquin and not Iroquois. Then armed bands of English and French roamed over its territory, which was claimed both by New Hampshire and by New York. Probably the first English settlement was Fort Dummer, built near the city of Brattleboro in 1724. The question as to who owned the land in the Green Mountain region was not settled until after the Revolution.

Thus the Eastern colonies on or near the Atlantic seacoast were begun by the Pilgrims and built up by the Puritans. In overwhelming majority the people were British, and most of this majority were English who came largely from the eastern, middle, and southern counties of England, though all of the shires were represented.

Whatever the faults of the Puritans may have been, they have left their ineffaceable stamp upon our national history. They had an intense conviction of the truth as they saw it, a clear idea of the authority of righteousness, a profound assurance of God's just and holy rule, and a deep sense of the dignity of man. They lacked interest in things æsthetic. They were contemptuous of some of the minor elegances of life. They were wanting in sympathy with questioning minds. Often they were unlovely and unattractive in their methods. The records of their courts and churches show that hypocrisy was common, and that their average ethical practice was sufficiently far from their theory.

Nevertheless, there were magnificent qualities in the Puritan spirit, such as its masterful sincerity, its majestic ideal, its superb and shining courage, its triumphant disregard of institutions, its clearest vision of things celestial and eternal.

Such a concentration of intellect, education, and homes in the Eastern colonies produced in colonial times and later its due results. Until our great Civil War, New England was almost a nation, and a noble one, in itself. Her sons and daughters have profoundly influenced the nation by their intellect, literary abilities, and enterprise. In education and in moral reforms, Massachusetts led all the colonies and states, and the brightest names in American literature are those of her children.

CHAPTER XIII.

MARYLAND AND CATHOLIC LIBERALITY.

THE church by law established in England was peculiar in many respects. When the Reformation aroused Europe from the intellectual slumbers of the middle ages, the Latin nations held to the Roman ideas, systems, and religion. The Germanic nations, revising their doctrines, ritual, and church order, instituted national Reformed churches.

Wherever the Reformation was led by the people, the tone of the church was democratic; where it was directed by the Puritans, it was aristocratic; where, as in England, it was ordered by the monarch, the state-church bishops were lords of the realm. The Reformed church of Holland, for example, was intensely democratic. The Lutheran church in Germany was ruled by the princes and their advisers. In England the bishops, who were appointees of the king and were even called lords bishops, had greater power than in any other Protestant country. In Scotland, Wales, and North Ireland the democratic spirit prevailed.

To secure the union of State and Church in England, persecution was used, and it is hard to tell whether the Puritans or the Catholics suffered the most; for both were heavily fined unless they attended the services of the church of England. Such coercion in the end proved of little benefit; for although based on force, the Established Church has to-day only a minority of English and only a small fraction of Welsh people within her pale, while in Ireland it has been reduced to a level with the other denominations. In the British colonies, the sect which in England is subsidized by the state is simply one among many, just as in the United States, where all varieties of religion must show their fitness to live by righteousness and not by dependence upon the sword or the public treasury. The Dutch republic first, as our constitutional fathers confessed, and the United States of America next, have been the leaders in demonstrating that religion is better off when it is voluntary and let alone by the state.

The Plymouth Pilgrims were not the only ones to get away from such a persecuting church. It was not they alone who were Pilgrims. The Catholics suffered terribly. George Calvert, called Lord Baltimore, an English Catholic nobleman, looked to America to find a refuge for his fellow-worshippers who were harried in England. Being in favor with King Charles I., his sovereign granted him a tract of land in northern Virginia, which was named Maryland. Geography was not well understood in those days, for even the coast-line had been but little measured and mapped out. This grant of Mary's land — for the French queen of Charles, Henrietta-Marie, gave her name to the new country — included, in addition to the territory of the Maryland of to-day, Delaware, part of Pennsylvania, and West Virginia.

All the Southern colonies were named after British sovereigns, — Virginia from the virgin Queen Elizabeth; Maryland from Mary Stuart, the wife of King Charles I.; the two Carolinas after Charles II.; and Georgia after King George II. Although Lord Baltimore died before the charter was signed, his son Cecil Calvert received the patent and, having great powers, carried on the work. In the spring of 1634 he sent out a colony of three hundred people, who crossed the ocean in the first section of a fleet under the command of the Dutch Admiral Van Bibber, from whom some of the best families in Maryland are descended. The ships were named the *Ark* and the *Dove*, the former being a large vessel of three hundred and fifty tons and the latter a pinnace of but fifty tons.

The company of "gentlemen adventurers" and their servants left Gravesend and stopped at the Isle of Wight, where two Jesuit fathers, White and

Altham, with some of the other emigrants were taken on board. Leaving Cowes November 22, 1633, they followed the old route, by the Azores and the West Indies, reaching Point Comfort February 27, 1634. Meeting the Indians, they assured them of their desire to impart the arts of civilization and to teach them the way to heaven. Considering that the aborigines had some rights to the soil, they bought thirty miles of the land from them for hatchets and cloth, and thus established their colony with the good will of the red men.

On the 27th of March, 1634, amid the firing of the ships' cannon, the emigrants disembarked from the *Ark* and began their new home. The Indians at once taught the white strangers the mysteries of woodcraft, to hunt the deer, to plant and use the chief American grain, to cook corn meal, and to make first-rate cakes and succotash. The Englishmen were so fortunate in their agriculture, that in this same year they raised a crop of maize, which they were able to send to Massachusetts to exchange for salt fish and other provisions. The Jesuit fathers set up the first Roman Catholic church in America, and began preaching the gospel among the Indians. Under their teachings many of the Protestants also, who were the laborers or servants in the colony, became Catholics. When Tayac, chief of the Piscataquas, was baptized, Governor

Calvert and the principal men of the colony were present at the ceremony.

The original colony consisted of twenty men of property or social standing, and the rest were wage-earners or dependents; but all of them took part in making the laws, and, in a few years, they had the power of originating them. The Assembly was composed of sixteen members, — nine burgesses or representatives, six councillors, and a governor, — and they entered upon their duties in 1649. Six were of the Reformed and eight were of the Roman form of the Christian faith, that of the others not being certain.

The very first law passed was one guaranteeing religious liberty. It set forth that no person " Professing to believe in Jesus Christ shall from thenceforth be in any wise troubled, molested, or discountenanced, for, or in respect of his or her religion, nor in the free exercise thereof within this Province . . . nor in any way compelled to the belief or exercise of any other religion against his or her consent." Thus, one of the first of the colonies to grant entire freedom of conscience was that under a Roman Catholic proprietor. In the same year, Governor Stone invited the Puritans who had been banished from Virginia to settle in Maryland. They came, and named the place where they settled Providence, on the site of Annapolis.

Thus nobly did Maryland follow the example of the country of Admiral Van Bibber, though the Marylanders fell far behind the Dutch in restricting their toleration or their grant of religious liberty to Christians who must be either Roman or Reformed; for their laws did not protect Jews and those who rejected the divinity of Christ.

The colonists had many troubles. Clayborne the Virginian held Cat Island in Chesapeake Bay, and would not leave until driven out by force. The Civil War, which divided the English people at home, compelled those in Maryland to array themselves on hostile sides, either for the Protector or Pretender. Clayborne's Rebellion kept the country disturbed during the better part of three years. The bold and unscrupulous Captain Ingle seized the colony in the name of the Puritan parliament of England, and sent home the aged Jesuit Father White in irons. When the Commonwealth was established, its commissioners in Maryland acted in a most intolerant manner, allowing no Catholics to have a seat in the legislature. They repealed the statute of toleration and prohibited Catholic worship. The old story of the poor cony that invited the hedgehog into its hole on a rainy day, only to be driven out, was enacted over again. The name of Puritan was disgraced by bigotry and intolerance.

In 1658 Lord Baltimore was reinvested with his rights, and freedom of worship again restored. Then the colony became fairly prosperous. Tobacco was cultivated and became the chief export. It was even used like money, at a penny a pound. In spite of the determination of the British government to repress manufactures, there were eight copper furnaces and nine forges in operation by 1750. Some wine was also produced. Both land and sea food were abundant, and the eastern shore became early famous for its oysters, terrapin, canvas-back ducks, and other delicacies. A generous hospitality and a society rich in social graces have ever characterized Maryland.

Thus the Catholics in Maryland and in our nation, in spite of their occasional blunders in politics, have always shown themselves in living sympathy with what is truly American. Reading the future by the past, we may be sure that, in time of foreign invasion or internal commotion, our government and nation may always rely upon their strong right arm. Slowly and surely the Catholics in the United States have progressed to a broad liberality, in spite of hostile secret organizations based on uncharitableness and injustice. The beginnings of Maryland were prophetic.

CHAPTER XIV.

THE CAROLINAS.

THE English people in the seventeenth century, especially after so many thousands of the best of them had emigrated to America, were not prepared for a republic; for they were not at that time educated up to the idea. When Cromwell died, there was no one to take his place and do his work. His son Richard proved a weak ruler, and soon the way was made ready in England by partisans of the Stuarts for the return of the monarchy, in 1660.

The new king, Charles II., had taken refuge in the Netherlands, where he was kindly treated, though he afterwards repaid the kindness of the Dutch by the foulest treachery. After the Royalist party had regained authority, Charles appointed Edward Hyde, one of his faithful followers, Lord Chancellor of England and Prime Minister. In 1661 this man, known as the Earl of Clarendon, who afterwards wrote what he called a history of "the rebellion," interested himself in the work of colonizing America. In 1663 he and his associates formed a company, to which Charles granted the vast territory lying south of Virginia. Retaining the name Carolina, which Charles IX. of France had given to the region when the Huguenots settled there in the previous century, they considered that they were getting all the land stretching westward to the Pacific Ocean and from Virginia to the tip of Florida.

General Monk, the chief agent in the restoration of the Stuarts and who was usually known in his day as " Old Monk," was made Duke of Albemarle. He it was who first clothed the British soldiers in scarlet, making them the famous " red coats " of whom we have heard so much, and whom our fathers met in the Revolutionary War. Like almost all leaders of the parliamentary army, he had fought under the banners of the Dutch republic. He served the king first, then Cromwell, and then the king again. He was in the Dutch pay early in life and later fought against them in command of an English fleet. His title-name has been given to Albemarle Sound. The name of another member, Lord Shaftesbury, or Mr. Ashley-Cooper, was given to two rivers in South Carolina. Other members of the company were Craven, Colleton, Carteret, and two men named Berkeley.

The first colony, made up of settlers in Virginia, was called Albemarle and the second, composed largely of planters who came from the West Indies,

Clarendon. During the next four years few colonists came from England to Carolina, and most of the actual settlers were the Huguenots or Christians of the Reformed church of France. In 1670 a body of these excellent people, who had come in two ships, landed much further south, forming the city of Charleston, which they named in honor of the king. After the Revocation of the Edict of Nantes in 1685, a still larger host of Huguenots settled in Carolina. This act of the bigoted Bourbon, Louis XIV., drove out of France five hundred thousand of the best people of the nation, impoverishing the country, but enriching Germany, Holland, England, and America. France paid dearly for her tyrant's folly. About one-half of the soldiers in the splendid army of William of Orange, which marched into London in 1688, to drive out Louis' ally, James II., were Huguenots. In 1871, in the German army of invasion, six hundred officers and thousands of privates were descendants of the French exiles of 1685.

From the very beginning, the company had granted religious liberty to all colonists, and this attracted many people of various nationalities, not only from Europe, but from other parts of America. The ship *Phœnix*, from New York, brought Germans, who built Jamestown on the Stone River. English, Irish, Scottish, French, Swiss, and more

Germans came to settle the new country. All Christians lived harmoniously together, until Lord Granville began his ruinous course of bigotry. He attempted to remove the religious privileges of the colonists, by excluding all who were not members of the Anglican church from the colonial legislature. This abominable policy started the struggle between the proprietors and the people, which finally led to the loss of their title by the former.

Even before this, in 1670, Mr. Anthony Ashley-Cooper, afterwards Earl of Shaftesbury, a fierce persecutor of the Catholics, attempted a silly experiment. He persuaded his secretary, the English philosopher John Locke, to write a constitution for Carolina, which he and his friends believed to be the most perfect work of its kind in existence. Locke was a closet statesman, despite the fact that he wrote a book " On the Human Understanding," which is supposed to embody the philosophy of common sense. In reality, this constitution was rather like a fossil of feudalism. It was one of those ridiculous systems of government in which the common people, who are the real makers of government, had no vote and no rights, but in which the noblemen monopolized privilege and power. The colonial parliament was graded into four chambers, — proprietors, landgraves, caziques, and lords of manors. The people were only "leet-men" or serfs, attached to the soil like the old *adscripti glebæ* of the Roman empire. Even their very food and clothes were regulated by a paternal government.

This constitution never got very much further than the paper on which it was written. Certainly, people of Scottish descent could never live under it. After twenty years of vain attempts at enforcing it, the proprietors gave up the idea. The document is now an interesting relic known only to antiquarians.

Shaftesbury was but one of a long list of foolish and impractical members of the semi-feudal society of England, who have tried to make worn-out old-world notions work in America, and whose failures are legion.

The new colonists were very industrious. They cut down the forests, cleared the soil for plantations, experimented with seeds which they had brought from Europe, raised excellent cattle, built comfortable houses, opened trade with the Indians, and explored the country. They soon found it necessary to form military companies for defence against the hostile natives and the Spaniards in Florida. Along the sultry low country of the coast there was much malaria and consequent sickness, but gradually the people pushed into the interior to the high lands and to the healthier plateaus. This scattered the settlers and prevented the growth of large towns.

The great demand for naval stores in Europe gave the people plenty to do in the forest, making pitch, tar, rosin, and turpentine.

In 1672 Sir John Yeamans imported the first slaves from Africa into the Carolinas. Here the negroes found a congenial environment and multiplied. Their masters were very apt to name their black servants after classic heroes and gods of mythology, such as Pompey, Cæsar, Hannibal, Remus, and Jason. It was not all sweat and toil for poor Sambo. He, too, had his fun and romance and beguiled the hours of rest and the long night-hours with fairy stories as old as the Aryans. In the new Western world, the ancient African folk-lore, a mixture of the paganism of the jungle and of distorted Buddhism, took on new forms.

The typical Uncle Remus no longer told the ancient animal stories borrowed from India, Arabia, and Egypt in the old African way, but used the creatures and scenery closest to him. In this way grew up the tales about "Brer Rabbit" and the "Tar Baby." In substance, the story is the same in India and Japan. It does not seem difficult to recognize in the sticky creature of our southern coast forests the old imp of matted locks and snarled-up hair with which the Buddha once fought and to which he stuck fast. The story contains a parable almost as old as human nature. In due time the children of African pagans learned the story of infinite love. To-day the negro shares in the Christianity and civilization of the great republic, in which religion — its forms settled by conscience and not by edict — is all the purer for being free.

North Carolina is famous for its great forests of tar-bearing trees, which abound within fifty leagues of the coast. The production of turpentine, tar, pitch, and rosin, so necessary in the days of wooden ships, was a vital necessity to Great Britain; but similar experiments tried in the Mohawk valley by the Palatine Germans failed, because the famous " Georgia pine," the great tar-bearing tree of this continent, does not grow north of southern Virginia.

When, in 1693, a ship from Madagascar came in and the captain gave a bag of rice to the governor, a new era of agricultural industry and of commerce began. This Oriental grain, the bread-food of Asia, found in southern Carolina a soil exactly suited to it. The farmers planted the rice on the swampy lands, until by and by this cereal became the chief crop, the product being the best quality in the world. South Carolina became a large botanic garden and experimental station on a large scale. Many new plants were offered a home in the new soil, among others indigo, which formerly had been raised only in Asia. This also was found to be admirably suited to the fertile and marshy land, and became a standard crop. In the markets of Europe the blue coloring matter brought over a dollar a pound. Indigo was followed by cotton, which, after the invention of the cotton gin, became even more lucrative, making South Carolina one of the richest of the Southern colonies and Charleston the metropolitan city of the South. Many young men were sent to Europe to be educated, while the name of the colony, because of its large trade and good credit, was well and favorably known in many countries.

The palmetto tree, both for utility and sentiment, is the tree of South Carolina. From the tender leaves of one sort may be made food and from the tough ones hats. With its logs, piers that defy the teredo mollusk and a fort that harmlessly absorbed British cannon-balls have been built. Another species, as being the congenial home of rattlesnakes, became the emblem on the colonial flag of the Palmetto State, though another flag had the coiled reptile itself with the legend, "Don't tread on me."

In 1729 the colony was divided into North Carolina and South Carolina. Then it ceased to be governed by proprietors and, being under direct control of the king, became a royal province. The Carolinas were the first of the twin colonies to separate, as the Jerseys were the first pair of colonies of the same name to unite and be known as one region and community.

CHAPTER XV.

GEORGIA, THE LAST OF THE THIRTEEN COLONIES.

GEORGIA was the last of the five Southern colonies settled. Its first beginning was not until the days of the generation just before the Revolutionary War. It was a period of great financial distress in England. Thousands of men were out of employment and the prisons were full of debtors. The law then was that if a man owed even a few pence, he could be put in jail. There he could save himself from starvation only by the help of his friends, or by begging through the bars of the cage in which he was kept. John Howard, the Baptist sheriff of Bedfordshire, had not yet come to reform the prisons of England, which were then a disgrace to civilization and far below the standard of Christianity on the Continent.

There was a military officer named James Edward Oglethorpe, who had served in the Netherland campaigns under the Duke of Marlborough. He had no doubt seen how much better the prisoners were treated on the Continent and certainly in Hol-

land. Returning from the wars, he spent much
time among the prisons of London, and his heart
was touched. When he saw such widespread mis-
ery, he determined to do something to give these
poor wretches a new start in life. America then,
as now, meant opportunity. His scheme met with
favor from the British government, which was then
under a new dynasty, — that of German princes
named Guelph, from Hanover. Under the patron-
age of King George II. a fund was started to which
private individuals generously subscribed, making a
sum equal to more than half a million dollars in
present values. It was also thought that if placed
further south than the Carolinas, the new colony
would help to protect those provinces from Spanish
invasion.

An association of twenty-two persons was formed,
of which General Oglethorpe, then in the prime of
life, was made the president, and of which the Wesleys and Whitfield were members. The present state
of Georgia, named after King George II., is shaped
somewhat like New Hampshire, especially in having
a large inland hilly area with but a few miles of
seacoast. It was hoped that in the new region both
wine and silk could be produced in large quantities.
The ship *Anne* left England November 17, 1732,
the same year in which Washington was born, having one hundred and thirty persons, in thirty-five

families, among whom were carpenters, brick-layers, farmers, and mechanics.

These first builders of a new commonwealth were well equipped with arms, tools, munitions, and stores. General Oglethorpe accompanied them. Sailing by way of Madeira, they entered the Savannah River, and made friendship with the Yamakraw Indians, through Mary Muskgrove, the daughter of a Canadian trader by an Indian mother. She persuaded the natives of the friendly intentions of the colonists, and secured from them an informal cession of the land. Thus, through a woman's tact and friendly offices, the way of success was made clear.

Early in February, the colonists began to mark out the squares and lots of the beautiful city of Savannah, Oglethorpe working hard among them every day. He also won the friendship of the Indians, and in May, 1733, invited them to the new settlement. A treaty was made May 21, by which the Creek Indians ceded to the whites a large tract of territory, and for many years the whites and the reds lived together like brothers. Equally with Oglethorpe should honor be awarded to Tomo-chi-chi, who was a Mico, or chief of chiefs, the guide and protector of the founders of Georgia.

Many of the Palatine Germans and Swiss had already settled in the Carolinas. Now into Georgia came Germans from further east, besides many of the Moravians. In the Austrian Salzburg, prelatical bigotry, which in 1498 had expelled the Jews and for centuries riveted the chains of despotism upon the people, had become unbearable to the Lutherans. Thirty thousand of these Bible-reading Christians, driven from their homes, had fled into Holland and England. Being invited to settle in Georgia, they took the oath of allegiance to the British king, and crossed the Atlantic Ocean. In March 1734, the ship *Purisburg*, having on board seventy-eight Salzburgers with their ministers, arrived in the colony. Warmly welcomed, they founded the town of Ebenezer.

It is interesting to notice how many towns in the United States have been named, not after the saints or churchly persons, but in recognition of the direct blessing of God. Note the Biblical or early Christian ideas, words, or characters, such as Philadelphia, Bethlehem, Nazareth, Salem, Providence, Sharon, Ebenezer, and Pella. Wherever people from the Latin nations settled in America, the names of saints abound.

The next year, more of these sober, industrious, and strongly religious people of Germany came over. The Moravians, who followed, quickly began missionary work among the Indians. After these came the Scotsmen, who, under Lieutenant Hugh

Maclay, had been recruited from the Highlands of old Scotia. They were brave men of excellent character, numbering one hundred and thirty, with fifty women and children, and were led by their own clergyman, Rev. John McLeod of the Island of Skye. With their plaids and their broadswords, their targets and muskets, these manly countrymen of Bruce and Wallace were just the men to ward off Spanish invasion. After them, again, followed German Lutherans, Moravians, English emigrants, Scotch-Irish Quakers, Mennonites, and others. Thus in Georgia, as in the Carolinas and Virginia, there was formed a miniature New Europe, having a varied population, with many sterling qualities. The history of England was repeated in the blending of races, and with the same result, — the production of an admirable stock, from which have sprung a remarkable number of men and women of eminent ability.

There was great popular discontent at first, because the colony had been placed on a military or feudal basis. The regulations of the company did not allow self-government, or the holding of land by women, or the importation of liquor or of slaves. These repressive rules prevented competition with other colonies, while the ban against Roman Catholics showed that entire religious liberty was not yet known in Georgia. The Wesleys,

John and Charles, visited the colony, but were not much encouraged, for their success was indifferent; but Whitfield succeeded in establishing an orphan asylum near Savannah. By his influence slavery was introduced and laws were passed which allowed a better land tenure and removed restrictions, thus greatly improving commerce. The colonists defended themselves with wisdom and valor against the Spaniards. In 1752 the colony became a royal province. From the first it was noticed that there were great riches in beds of coal and iron. Later on, cotton made Georgia one of the wealthiest of the colonies in natural products, besides leading in the trade with the West Indies.

CHAPTER XVI.

WILLIAM PENN AND THE JERSEYS.

NEW NETHERLAND included all the land on which now rest the four Middle states of the Union, besides part of Connecticut and Massachusetts, the Hudson River and Lake Champlain region, and the unexplored territory westward. What is now New Jersey was first occupied by Dutch inhabitants in 1617. The traders of Manhattan Island crossed over the river and at a place which they called the Hills, or Bergen, they erected a fortified trading-post. Then moving to the southwest, they built a house for business and defence at Gloucester, on the river opposite the site of Philadelphia. Between 1614 and 1621, there was considerable traffic in furs. After the regular settlers had begun agriculture and the patroons settled their manors, there were Dutch farms, shipyards, and trading stations.

When the treacherous attack in time of peace was made on New Netherland by the Duke of York, this ignoble man transferred the whole territory lying between the Delaware and the Hudson to two of his friends, Lord John Berkeley and Sir George Carteret. The latter had been governor of one of the Channel Islands, a part of old Normandy and the home of the Alderney cows. It is named Jersey, which is only a corruption of Cæsarea. In compliment to Carteret's loyalty, the Duke of York, who was to be the next king of England, named the new possessions which he had treacherously gained, " New Jersey." The wits afterwards dubbed him, when James II., the " ape of Cæsar." In honor of Lady Elizabeth Carteret, the first comers under his rule, who were mostly from England, named their settlement Elizabethtown, or, as now called, Elizabeth.

The people were granted a direct voice in the government, and the general political provisions were made with a liberality that attracted even more emigrants from the Eastern colonies than from Great Britain. At Shrewsbury, Middletown, and on other sites were soon thriving towns. One party coming from England made a home on the banks of the Passaic River and began the city of Newark. They set up a Congregational church, and declared that none but church members should be freemen of the town or have a vote.

Difficulties arose between Governor Nichols of New York and the proprietors of New Jersey over land titles, and the settlers could not tell who was their true landlord. When Governor Nichols determined to form an independent government, the old governor and council of New Jersey, finding it impossible to enforce their authority, went over to England to appeal to the Duke of York, who declared the grants under the authority of Nichols to be void.

The next year Lord Berkeley, discouraged at the management of affairs, sold his one-half interest in the province for less than five thousand dollars to John Fenwick and Edward Billinge. When the new proprietors got in dispute about the division of their property, William Penn arbitrated the difficulty to the satisfaction of all. In 1675 Fenwick, with his family and a small company of Friends, sailed from London in the ship *Griffith*, which means Great Faith. Entering the Delaware Bay, they landed on the banks of the creek. In gratitude to God and in love to the Prince of Peace, they named their settlement Salem. This was the first permanent English colony established in West Jersey. For a long time this region was spoken of as " The Jerseys," or, as people then pronounced it, " The Jarseys." Under the Friends, self-government and religious liberty were enjoyed and many industries, including manufactures, begun; but the trouble about land titles never ceased until the proprietors put the two colonies under the British crown.

Then New Jersey was united in government to New York, not becoming a separate province until 1738.

In the building up of a country, the people are more important than institutions. In the making of a commonwealth, men are more than measures. Some writers pay attention only to the political side of history, telling us about princes and politicians, documents and charters, but seeming almost to forget race traits, characteristics, the influence of soil, natural features, and climate, and divine Providence. Yet politics show but one side of man's nature, and the doings of kings and their favorites are often of far less importance than the people whom they serve or govern. In the making of a country like ours, we must not forget either the splendid quality of the different nationalities, or the social forces, or the ancestral influences that made our fathers what they were. It is well to remember that the women as well as the men, the mothers as well as the fathers, had a part in guiding the history which made our nation.

In Europe the British nations were not the only ones engaged in the struggle for liberty. Indeed, in the seventeenth century, Holland led the van of freedom and in the little Dutch republic were trained many of the colonial leaders and founders of commonwealths. Indeed, we may say the majority of those who began the colonies north of Maryland were educated and powerfully influenced in those Dutch United States which were the forerunner in history of the American Commonwealth.

Margaret Jasper, the daughter of John Jasper of Amsterdam, a Dutch lady, married Admiral Sir William Penn, the conqueror of Jamaica. Her son William Penn was born on Tower Hill, in London, October 14, 1644. He inherited the features and the disposition of his mother, as well as her native language and the noblest traits of the Dutch character. His mother trained him, and instilled in him the best traditions of her race and country. He saw comparatively little of his father, who was most of the time at sea, engaged in the British naval service. In Chester cathedral, the visiting American can sit and worship to-day under British flags which once waved in the valleys of the Hudson and Delaware, and under the armor of Admiral Penn.

The boy Penn was sent to Christ Church College, Oxford. George Fox, who taught doctrines very much the same as those of the Dutch Mennonites, was at this time setting forth the views and founding the denomination of Christians called " Friends." Under the preaching of Thomas Lee, who was called a " Quaker," William Penn embraced the peaceful doctrines of the Friends. He would not attend the college services, and was there-

fore expelled from the University; for all "chapel
services" were then obligatory.   His angry father
next sent him to Paris, hoping that the impressions
made by the Quaker preacher would be effaced in
the gayety of the French capital.   In Paris, Penn
studied for a while under a professor, in the French
Reformed church, and then travelled in France and
Italy.   When he came back to England, the dread-
ful scenes of the plague in London made him very
serious again.   To overcome this state of mind, his
worldly father sent him to Ireland, where in an in-
surrection among the soldiers, at Carrick Fergus
Castle, the admiral's son served in its suppression as
a volunteer under Lord Arran.   It was at this time
that the portrait which represents William Penn,
in armor, a young man of twenty-two, was painted.
In Ireland, Penn again came under the influence of
the Friends' preacher Lee, and suffered arrest at
a " Quaker meeting."   This experience again alienated his father, who relented when he found out
how sincere in convictions his son was.

Penn now began to write industriously in defence
of his views and to obtain toleration in behalf of the
Quakers.   Charged with heresy, he was imprisoned in the Tower, where he wrote the book, " No
Cross, No Crown."   Again released and again imprisoned, he penned, while behind bars, " The Great
Cause of Liberty of Conscience Debated."

The prison, as in all history, proved to be one of the best places for the making of good books, some of the world's noblest literature, including a large portion of the Bible, having been written behind bars by men who were convicts but not criminals. William Penn would have been a great man and well remembered in our day, even if he had done nothing more than write, but his prison experience made him a statesman also. Reflection led him to think that the dreams and plans of Sir Thomas More, author of the wonderful book called "Utopia," and of James Harrington, who penned "The Commonwealth of Oceana," could be realized upon the solid earth. The cathedral exists in the brain, and the plans on paper, before delver, mason, roofer, or artist does his part. So in all ages, noble men, who are the architects of progress, have built up civilization in thought first, before they or others have actually begun by work of hand to realize it in substance.

Sir Thomas More, the intimate friend of Erasmus, the Rotterdammer, had in his "Utopia," or Nowhere, written an account of an imaginary commonwealth in a distant island of the Atlantic, of which the manners, laws, and state of society were depicted as models worthy of English imitation. This political romance concerning "The Happy States of the Republic, and the New Island of Nowhere," written

in Latin and printed on the Continent, in 1516, ex-
cited universal admiration. Except Venice on the
waters and Switzerland in the mountains, republics,
even when imaginary, had to be located out in the
distant sea, the far Atlantic.

James Harrington, born five years before the
death of Shakespeare, was an Oxford student who,
as soon as he had travelled in Holland, began to be
interested in problems of government. He served
in the Dutch war for freedom, imbibed republican
ideas. He was much at The Hague, and familiar
with the court of the Prince of Orange. He then
visited Italy. Seeing how well republicanism, both
in Holland and at Venice, had prospered, he became
deeply interested in political science. On his return
to England, he wrote out his wonderful dream of
the future called " Oceana." This book, by an en-
thusiastic republican, is the description of an ideal
republic, and is dedicated to Oliver Cromwell.
Harrington's " Oceana " expresses his hope of that
England to come which we, in our day, see and
which is yet coming. It is full of fancy and of
common sense, and cautiously written so as not to
excite suspicion. In it we see a great deal of what
is now commonplace and matter of fact, both in
England and the United States of America.

"Oceana" had a great influence on the mind of
William Penn, who determined to put the ideas of

More and Harrington in practice. He went over to his mother's home land, becoming greatly interested in federal government and the Dutch civilization. Returning, honored and trusted, he was called on to arbitrate and to gain much experience in settling the quarrels between Fenwick and Billynge, about their possessions in New Jersey. After his release from imprisonment and the publication of his book on Liberty of Conscience, Penn travelled again through Holland and Friesland and in Germany. He talked with and preached to the Dutch in their own language, winning many converts to the doctrine of the Friends. In Friesland, he was struck with the democratic spirit of the people and the forms of their government, some of the features of which he afterwards introduced into New Jersey and Pennsylvania.

Penn made a second missionary journey to the Continent in company with George Fox, Robert Barclay, and George Keith. Besides preaching to the Dutch in his mother's tongue, he visited Rotterdam and many Holland towns, and went again into Frisia, where the language is so much like English. He also travelled through Hanover, Germany, and the Lower Rhine, making a special impression upon the Dutch and German Mennonites, the forerunners of the Friends. Those from Crefeld had a large part in the settlement of Germantown in Pennsylvania. Those who came from Kircheim are noted as the first in America to declare it unlawful for Christians to hold slaves.

Returning to his home, Penn pleaded with pen and tongue that England should grant the same toleration to the Friends which he had seen common to all sects in the Netherlands. But toleration for " Dissenters " then seemed as far off as ever and the future of English politics under King Charles II. hopeless. Penn therefore turned his eyes to America, determined to carry out his experiment of "a godly commonwealth" where conscience should be as free as in Holland, and where the ideas of prison reform which he had got from the same country, and the political privileges, making men as free as in " Free Frisia," should become reality.

CHAPTER XVII.

PENN'S EXPERIMENT OF A GODLY COMMONWEALTH.

PENN had been fined for not removing his hat in court, but he was released in time to be present at his father's death on September 16, 1670. He then found himself in possession of a fortune yielding an income of fifteen hundred pounds a year, besides a claim on the crown of fifteen thousand pounds lent by his father to Charles II.

Knowing of this royal debt, and thinking it might be commuted in American lands, Penn applied, June 24, 1680, "for a tract of land in America north of Maryland, bounded on the east by the Delaware, on the west limited as Maryland, northward as far as plantable." This meant a territory three hundred by one hundred and fifty miles in dimensions, very fertile and rich in mineral wealth. He suggested the name Sylvania, but the king added the name Penn in honor of the late admiral. Although Penn strenuously objected, he could not get the name changed, and so he became lord of Pennsylvania.

The " Groves of Penn," fronting on the Delaware River and containing nearly fifty thousand square miles, were in area as large as the whole of England. Penn now sent word to his friends in Scotland, Germany, and the Dutch states and encouraged the formation of the society of the " Free Society of Traders in Pennsylvania " and other adventurers. A party of pioneers was sent out in 1681. Penn then drew up a body of conditions and concessions. This constitution savored strongly of Harrington's " Oceana," but also borrowed very much that was actually in practical working in the Dutch republic, especially in Friesland. It was democratic in the purest sense. A council of seventy-two was chosen by universal suffrage every three years, one-third retiring each year, after the Dutch manner. Having written to the Indians inviting their friendship, Penn sailed with a hundred of his comrades from Deal, in the ship *Welcome*, September 1, 1682. Small-pox broke out on board, and one-third of the passengers died. This was a hundred years before Dr. Jenner and vaccination.

When Penn landed at New Castle, Delaware, October 27, he was welcomed by the Swedes and Dutch already settled there, and received formal possession.

The ceremonies of transfer, which took place in the presence of nearly the whole white population

WILLIAM PENN TAKING FORMAL POSSESSION OF PENNSYLVANIA.

of Pennsylvania, who assembled as witnesses, were borrowed from the Dutch. A sod was cut from the ground with a spade and handed to William Penn, significant of the fact that he was lord of the whole territory, owning the land and all that grew on it. Then a drinking vessel, filled with Delaware River water, was offered him, which signified that he owned the water as well as the bottom of the river. In the third place, a key of the fort was put in his charge, completing the transfer, and signifying that he had the right of holding both land and water by force.

The Assembly met at once, and, on the 7th of December passed " The great law of Pennsylvania." This, one of the noblest of the colonial constitutions, showed that Pennsylvania was to be a Christian state on the model of the Friends, who had not a single musket among them, or firearms of any sort. Only one condition was made necessary for citizenship or office: namely, Christianity. All offices were elective, and the general order was purely democratic. Monopolies were not allowed. The penalty of death, for all offences except murder, was abolished.

Penn had great faith in the principles of arbitration. He believed that the Scripture exhortation, " Let the peace of God arbitrate in your hearts," could be carried out in practice, not only among individuals, but even between states. While in the Netherlands, he had been impressed with the unity, power, and peace-

fulness of a republic in which there were manifold
sources of authority. There were cities with their
municipal charters, noblemen with their manors,
states with their legislatures, and the general national government at The Hague. Here was unity
amid diversity — *e pluribus unum* — besides social
harmony among men of all kinds of religious belief,
— Jews, Agnostics, Unitarians, Trinitarians, Lutherans, Calvinists, Arminians, and Mennonites, living quietly in peace. Later on, having successfully
carried out his principle in Pennsylvania, he wrote
"A Plan for the Peace of Europe," in which he puts
forth the idea of a great court of arbitration, like that
which is being attempted in this our day, under
the administrations of Presidents Cleveland and
McKinley. Though the vision tarry, Penn was a
true prophet, as well as a follower of the Prince of
Peace, who took Jesus seriously.

His frame of government for the white settlers
having been formed, Penn gathered the Lenni-
Lenape aborigines, who belonged to the Algonquin
group of tribes. These Delaware River Indians
and others assembled under a great elm tree at
Shackamaxon, the native name of the suburb of
Philadelphia afterwards called Kensington. Fifty
years of kind treatment at the hands of the Swedes
and Dutch, both of whom had paid for their lands
and traded honestly, had smoothed the way for the

Friends, who had no trouble with their red brethren. Without any oath and with mutual frankness, a covenant of friendship was entered into, " never sworn to and never broken." For sixty years, so long as the Friends had control of the government, this compact was never violated.

In Indian custom, the document, equivalent to our engrossed parchment record, with signatures solemnly attested by a great seal of wax held by ribbons, was a belt of wampum. This was handed to Penn with eloquent speeches and solemn ceremonies. It consisted of long strings of white shells, varied with three oblique bands of black. Wrought in the centre are two figures, of a bareheaded Indian and a white man with a hat on, who are clasping hands in token of friendship. The old tree grew near the banks of the Delaware, not far away from where the later " Free Quakers " and shipbuilders, Manuel and Jehu Eyre, launched the first gunboats for the Continental Congress. The monument on its site — for it was blown down in 1811 — stands near the great shipyard, in which the splendid steel battle-ships of our modern United States navy have been constructed and launched by the Cramps.

Penn laid out the capital city, according to a plan which he had borrowed from Babylon and had elaborated before leaving England. The streets were to run north and south and east and west.

Those between the two rivers, the Delaware and Schuylkill, were numbered in consecutive order, from Front or First Street to the Fourteenth or Broad, and beyond. Those running east and west were called after the trees of the forest, Chestnut, Walnut, Spruce, Pine, etc., and the fruits, Mulberry, Raspberry, etc. He named his new city Philadelphia, or Brotherly Love, its motto being that of the first verse of the thirteenth chapter of Hebrews — *Philadelphia Maneto*, "Let brotherly love continue." The city grew very rapidly, and within two years contained three hundred houses and a population of twenty-five hundred. People of the four British nations and Swedes, Germans, Dutch, and Swiss poured rapidly into the new province. Later on, with the coming of the Ulstermen, the population in forty-eight years, from 1701 to 1749, increased over twelvefold, from twenty thousand to a quarter of a million souls.

At Germantown, settled by the Dutch and Germans, mostly Mennonites, new industries were introduced, especially the making of wine, the working of silk, and the weaving of linen. The town seal consists of a clover leaf, on one lobe of which is a bunch of grapes, on another a distaff of flax, and on another a spool of silk, with the motto, *Vinum, linum et textrinum*. Here lived Daniel Pastorius, then the most learned man in America.

Pennsylvania is sometimes called " The American German's Holy Land." Let us see why. To-day, as the tourist visits Heidelberg on the Neckar, or sails down the Rhine from Spires or Mannheim to Cologne, he sees many ivy-mantled ruins, which show how terribly Louis XIV. of France desolated this region during his ferocious wars. Angry at the Germans and Dutch for sheltering his hunted Huguenots, and at the British for deposing James II. and welcoming William III. of Holland, he invaded the Rhine Palatinate, which became for a whole generation the scene of French fire, pillage, rapine, and slaughter. Added to these troubles of war and politics, were those of religious persecution; for, according as the prince electors were Protestant or Catholic, so the people were expected to change as suited their rulers, who compelled their subjects to be of the same faith. In the middle ages, and until the Dutch changed it, the formula was *ejus regio, cujus religio*, which meant that the prince ruled both land and conscience. Tired of their long-endured miseries, the Palatine Germans, early in the eighteenth century, fled to England. Under the protection and kindly care of the British government, they were aided to come to America. About five thousand settled in the Hudson, Mohawk, and Schoharie valleys in New York, and over twenty-five thousand in Pennsylvania, chiefly in the Schuylkill and Swatara region between Bethlehem and Harrisburg. Later came Germans from other parts of the Fatherland, making colonists rich in the sturdy virtues of the Teutonic race.

Though poor, these Germans were very intelligent, holding on to their Bibles and having plenty of schools and schoolmasters. In the little Mennonite meeting-house at Germantown, on the 18th of February, 1688, they declared against the unlawfulness of holding their fellow-men in bondage, and raised the first ecclesiastical protest against slavery in America. In Penn's colony also the first book written and published in America against slavery was by one of these German Christians. Anthony Benezet, who was a Huguenot Quaker and a schoolmaster, wrote tracts on religious liberty and against negro slavery. These powerfully stimulated the mind of William Wilberforce of England, the great philanthropist who opposed the war with America, and pleaded for the emancipation of Catholics and the abolition of slavery.

The Pennsylvania Germans also published the first Bible in any European tongue ever printed in America. It was they who first called Washington "the father of his country." In their dialect, still surviving in some places, made up of old German and modern expressions, some pretty poems and charming stories have been written. Tenacious in holding their lands, thorough in method, appreciative of most of what is truest and best in our nation's life, but not easily led away by mere novelties and justly distrustful of what is false and unjust, even though called "American," the Germans have furnished in our national composite an element of conservatism that bodes well for the future of the republic.

The central and western parts of Pennsylvania were later settled by Irish and Scottish people. Philadelphia grew so rapidly that at the end of colonial life, it was the largest and most important city in North America, the literary centre, and the place of the first beginning of schools for women. In its free atmosphere, Benjamin Franklin found his place of development. Here were the ablest lawyers, the first philosophic and scientific societies; here lived and worked the first American astronomer, Rittenhouse; and here originated many first things which have so powerfully influenced the nation at large. In many other ways Philadelphia has been a pioneer city.

CHAPTER XVIII.

NEW SWEDEN AND DELAWARE.

IN the era of discovery, Scandinavia and Italy were the two maritime countries of Europe that helped to unveil America, yet neither possessed any part of it. Even little Denmark owned Greenland, a small continent by itself, but with only a habitable strip of seacoast.

Sweden had sent no explorers to America in the sixteenth century, though half a millennium before the Norsemen had made voyages across the Atlantic and had begun settlements in North America. From these, however, the governments of Norway and Sweden made no claim of territory, any more than did the crown of England claim the Pacific coast because Sir Francis Drake had visited it.

The Dutch navigators first explored and mapped the coast of Delaware and entered its waters, giving their names to Capes May and Henlopen, which jut out from opposite points of land, forming the gateway to the noble bay. The later name of the colony came from the river, in which Lord de la Warr, the captain-general of Virginia, had at one time found shelter. The first actual settlement by De Vries, a Dutch commander whose name means "the Frisian," was made in 1630, near Lewes, where to-day is the great breakwater within which hundreds of ships and coasting vessels anchor for shelter during times of severe storm. De Vries' colony was destroyed by the Indians.

Gustavus Adolphus, the noble king of Sweden and the great leader of the forces of Reformed Christianity during the Thirty Years' War, had a great desire to plant a colony in America, and as early as 1627 plans were perfected for this purpose. Soon he was obliged to lead his army across the Baltic Sea, and being kept long in the tented field, his American enterprises had to bide their time. Gustavus Adolphus was killed at the battle of Lutzen in 1632, but his famous chancellor, Oxenstiern, carried out his lamented sovereign's desire. Peter Minuit entered the Swedish service, and in 1637, with a ship of war and a smaller vessel, he led a colony of Swedes and Finns, with their chaplain, to the Delaware River region, between Cape Henlopen and Christiana Creek. They bought land of the Indians and called the country New Sweden. By treaty, the land "ceded to the Swedish crown forever" extended from Christiana Creek to the falls of the Susquehanna River. At the mouth of the stream they built a fort and a house of worship, which was the first Lutheran church edifice on this continent. Their chief settlement, near the present city of Wilmington, was named Christiana, after the virgin Queen of Sweden. Minuit had to write the deed of transfer in Dutch, for none of the Indians understood Swedish. The savages made signature to the document with their marks or totems.

A second company of immigrants from Sweden, under Colonel John Printz, came over in 1642. Their chaplain, Campanius, at once proceeded to learn the tongue of the Delaware Indians, and after a while preached to them the gospel. Luther's Catechism was soon translated,— probably the first Protestant book in an American dialect,— though it was not printed until some years later. In 1669, on the pretty green slopes of Wicaco, within the limits of the later Philadelphia and near the Delaware River, the original of the present octagon stone edifice, "The Old Swedes' Church," was built of logs.

The Dutch considered the Swedes intruders, and built a fort at New Castle, five miles below them. In 1655 Governor Stuyvesant led an expedition, of seven ships with seven hundred men,. from Manhattan into the Delaware, and took possession of the country. Most of the Swedes, some of them settling in New Jersey and some in

Delaware, took the oath of allegiance to the Dutch republic. When, in 1664, the Duke of York conquered New Netherland, he claimed Delaware as belonging to him, but afterwards sold it to William Penn, though Lord Baltimore also claimed it. It was considered a part of Pennsylvania, but had its separate Assembly, and until the Revolution was always spoken of as "the three lower counties on the Delaware."

Most of the Swedes and Dutch remained under Penn's government, and were glad to do so. These Swedish Lutherans were the advance guard of a great host of Christian people in America who now number millions and are rich in churches, colleges, schools, education, the religious press, and in works of charity and missionary zeal. The disciples of Luther who come to this country are from many lands and speak various languages, but English is usually the tongue of the second generation in America. Within the present century a great host of Swedes and Norwegians have settled in the great Northwest.

Geography was not a science especially cultivated in Great Britain, and even the Royal Geographical Society was not founded until 1830. Nor was surveying very accurately done. So long as kings gave away, on parchment, vast tracts of territory, mensuration was in a rude state. Land

in gullies, swamps, stony areas, or not thought valuable was often neglected. The settlers "stepped off"
their ground or took lengths by means of poles,
ropes, or harness reins. In the west country beyond the coast, settlements were as yet unknown,
but even in the region between the mountains and
the sea-beach, there were many boundary disputes
between the colonial governments. Not only this,
but France, Spain, England, and the Netherlands
had much trouble and contention over their various
claims, and the alleged lines of demarcation.

Some of the wars fought on the American continent were over boundary lines, as many wars
often are yet. While nations are greedy and ambi-
tious, and some weak, and some strong, there will
always be a tendency to "rectify the frontier" in
ways not strictly righteous, — especially when it
is uncertain on which side gold mines, or fisheries,
or other sources of wealth may lie. The main
trouble is that, usually, diplomatists sitting in easy-
chairs in pleasant rooms prefer to settle such questions over a table with maps and pencils, instead
of having the work done by surveyors. From the
days of Prince Henry of Portugal and King Fer-
dinand of Spain, to our time of the Venezuela
Boundary Commission and the Klondike line, these
things have led to excitement and even war.

William Penn, besides giving the United States

of America other noted precedents and examples, showed how a boundary line ought to be made, — not by closet geographers or greedy diplomatists, each one eager to overreach the other, but by actual surveyors working on the ground between the earth and the stars, with instruments of precision and producing results wrought out by scholarly mathematicians. So, while courts and cabinets talked by the month, employed platoons of secretaries, over maps and documents, and fired bags of despatches at each other, the successors of William Penn rectified the blunder committed through royal ignorance of geography, and which had caused disputes for nearly a century.

The boundary between Pennsylvania and Delaware was agreed upon by the proprietors to be the arc of a circle, drawn with a radius of twelve miles from the court house at New Castle on the Delaware to the Maryland border. Arrangements were also made for a boundary west, and commissioners were appointed to run the lines. This was in 1732, the year in which Washington, the surveyor and engineer, was born. Chancery suits were the chief result of the imperfect work of 1739 and 1750. Then other commissioners were appointed. The surveyors began operations, and spent three years in measuring the line separating Delaware from Maryland.

The proprietors then selected the more skilled mathematicians, Messrs. Mason and Dixon, who verified the work of their predecessors, and ran the western line, beginning on November 6, 1763. They were stopped by the Indians in the summer of 1767, when 244 miles west of the Delaware, and only 36 miles east of the terminus they were seeking. Stones were erected at the intervals of a mile, and on every fifth stone, on its opposite sides, were engraved the arms of Lord Baltimore and William Penn. In 1782 the remainder of the boundary was completed and marked. This famous line became in the popular idea, especially in Europe, the demarcation between what later were known as the Northern and Southern or between the slave and the free states. The line fixed by the Missouri Compromise in 1820, however, was at 36° 30', while that between Maryland and Pennsylvania is at 39° 43' of north latitude.

When Delaware became an independent state, a blue flag with white stars was adopted as the sign of sovereignty. This flag was humorously spoken of as resembling "a speckled blue hen," and the people "The Blue Hen's Chickens." Delaware's colonial history falls under that of Pennsylvania, but as a state, its war-ships were the very first to salute the stars and stripes afloat. Delaware led the thirteen states in adopting the Constitution.

CHAPTER XIX.

GERMANIC OR LATIN CIVILIZATION IN NORTH AMERICA?

THREE great European powers struggled during two centuries for the control of North America. They were Spain, France, and Great Britain. So long as Spain was so fully occupied with South America, Mexico, and the West Indies, and especially while her best armies were being beaten by the Dutch republicans in fighting for their independence, there was little likelihood of her making good her claims to all America.

On the north the French and their allies, the Algonquin Indians, gave the Eastern colonists much anxiety in their early days, and later led to greater military expeditions. One of the first combinations was the New England Confederation. For mutual defence, the four colonies of Massachusetts Bay, Plymouth, Connecticut, and New Haven formed a league which lasted over forty years. Maine and Rhode Island desired to join the Union, but the former was refused because the worship of the church of England was maintained there, and the latter because religion was free.

It was the Plymouth men, who had lived under a federal government in the Dutch republic, who proposed this union. The model was evidently that of the States-General, both in detail and general procedure.

In all federal governments, it is a vital principle that each state or represented body, large or small, have equal representation ; but where one state, in population or wealth, is equal or nearly so to all the others combined, there is danger that the large and wealthy state will be greedy of too much power. So it happened in the Dutch League of Seven States, where the resources and population of Holland were nearly equal to those of the other six states combined. Hence there was constant danger from the ambition and power of one member of the confederacy that paid forty-eight per cent of all the taxes.

The New England Confederacy was formed in 1643, but in practice the same evils were encountered as in the Netherlands. Massachusetts was too large, and wanted things too much her own way. For about twenty years only did the Union have any real life, and it came to an end when Charles II. sent over Andros as governor, who trampled upon all law and carried out his master's wishes to perfection.

We shall see how, later, in 1690, after the massacre of Schenectady, under Jacob Leisler, and in 1740, at Albany, under Benjamin Franklin, further attempts at a union of colonies for mutual safety were made.

In 1647 Peter Stuyvesant was sent out as governor of New Netherland. A man of great energy, he made one of the best of Dutch governors. He was then forty-five years old and in the prime of life. He had served in the West Indies, where in the attack upon the Spanish island of St. Martin he lost a leg. Patent spring limbs being then unknown, he wore a wooden substitute, and this being handsomely ornamented with studs of silver, he was often called " Old Silver Nails," or " Old Silver Leg." He had been living three years in Holland before he was appointed director-general of New Netherland.

Soon after his arrival, he sent for Arendt Van Curler and took good counsel from him, and thus from the first treated the Indians with kindness and justice. Absolutely honest, not knowing what fear was, and intent on doing justice to all, he brought order into the colony. He was thoroughly faithful to his employers, conscientious in everything, and devoutly religious. He had a hot temper and strong will.

Stuyvesant's other virtues were not of the typical Dutch sort. He ruled in an aristocratic spirit.

Without much faith in popular government, he sided with the political ideas which in Holland have always been opposed to democracy. The Dutch farmers and traders in New Netherland had been used to much more freedom in their native country than either the patroons or the governors wished to allow. Stuyvesant tried hard to check the growing liberal spirit, but the popular demand asserted itself. A council of nine men was elected to assist the governor and to say how taxes should be raised and the money disbursed. Thereafter popular liberty steadily broadened in New Netherland. In this the Dutch were reasserting ancient rights; for their doctrine of "no taxation without consent" is as old as the middle ages. It was the rock on which Philip II. stumbled, and which, falling on Spain, nearly ground that proud Power to powder.

While his countrymen were broadening and deepening in religious liberty, Old Silver Nails held to the sectarian bigotry which had brought Barneveldt to the block. He was severe upon the Quakers, though he was not so horribly cruel as the Massachusetts Puritans. He was angry because the Anabaptists flourished. He fined the Lutheran churchmen and their supporters. Yet all this was so totally different from the spirit of brave little Holland, that, by the very next ship after that which

brought the news of a Dutchman's shameful conduct in imitating the kings and church lords of
Europe, Stuyvesant was severely rebuked. He was
given to understand that no man was to be persecuted for his faith, but that religious liberty must
be the rule in New Netherland, as well as in the
old country. From that time forth, there was no
trouble in the colony to any law-abiding citizen,
whatever his religious opinions might be.

In other respects, Stuyvesant made a capital
governor. Although in 1656 New Amsterdam had
only a thousand inhabitants, it was as cosmopolitan
as Greater New York now is. Though most of the
people were Dutch, there were many Walloons and
Huguenots, insular British folk of four sorts, and
Continental Europeans of many kinds, — a new
Europe in miniature. The laws had to be published
in three languages, and there were from fourteen to
twenty tongues spoken on Broadway, for the ships
of many nations came into the harbor for trade.
None better than the Dutch understood the advantages of this great gateway from the ocean into the
continent. Much firmness and wisdom were necessary to govern such a variety of people, especially
in a seaport where more strong drink was sold than
was necessary for comfort.

Stuyvesant also guarded against the encroachments of the Puritans in Connecticut upon the

limits of New Netherland, being most anxious, also, as a Christian magistrate, to keep the peace among white men in the presence of the Indians. Being peremptorily ordered to dispossess the Swedes on the Delaware, he captured the fort which the Swedish Governor Rising had taken in 1654, and took possession of the entire colony of New Sweden.

Ten years later, it was the turn of the biters to be bitten; for then the Dutch were themselves turned out by the British. By 1664 the English people in the Eastern colonies and in Virginia, who looked upon the Netherlanders as intruders, wanted to get them out and have English people in their place, while the British king was covetous of the rich land and splendid harbor which the Dutch had opened to civilization.

The Duke of York, whom history can call little less than a buccaneer, who had already needlessly ravaged Portuguese settlements in Africa, was very anxious to distinguish himself by capturing New Netherland. Charles II. determined to seize the country; but as he gave assurances to the Dutch government that he intended no such thing, and told many royal lies, the West India Company was lulled into security. As one of the great motives in founding the colony had been to weaken Spain, and as the Dutch had, as far back as 1648, humbled their great enemy and won their complete independence from the Spanish king, they paid little attention to their American province. The defences were neglected. The fort fell into disrepair. There was a garrison of only sixteen soldiers in the bastions, and there was not a single man-of-war in the harbor. Knowing the weakness and unguarded condition of Manhattan Island, the Stuart king at once improved his opportunity. Although it was a time of profound peace, the British government, in August, 1664, sent Colonel Nichols, with a fleet of ships and about a thousand soldiers, who demanded instant surrender.

The brave Stuyvesant showed fight and refused at first to yield; but finding few to second him, he appointed Domine Megapolensis and other citizens to treat with the British commander to secure protection of life and liberty. Excellent terms were made, by which freedom of conscience, trade, and representative government were guaranteed. The province was named New York, and the city likewise. Nichols at once sent for Arendt Van Curler to gain over the Iroquois Indians and to secure the frontiers, and took the good advice of this leader and statesman.

Stuyvesant visited Holland to give account to the company of his stewardship, but came back to spend the remainder of his life on his farm, or " bowery," in that part of the city which still retains its name. At the time of the surrender, there were probably not over ten thousand white people in the whole region where now New York, New Jersey, Pennsylvania, and Delaware have now a population of fifteen millions. It is quite possible that one-half of the Netherlanders returned home, not liking English ways of government; so that in all New York there were probably not more than five thousand Netherlanders remaining. From these have sprung that excellent stock which has been so powerful in making New York the Empire State, and in helping to settle the West. Their descendants, among whom are so many heroes, legislators, authors, inventors, and men eminent in all the departments of life, have spread all over the Union.

The English governor, Colonel Nichols, was a man of energy and good sense. After him came Francis Lovelace, who was not a particularly interesting character. When, in 1674, war broke out again between the Dutch and English, for the possession of the seas, Admiral Cornelius Evertse, flying the flag of the republic, came into the harbor of New York and recaptured the city and province. Then, to the great joy of many inhabitants, followed a year of Dutch rule; but the English Parliament compelled King Charles to cease war with Holland and to make peace.

The region of New Netherland again came under English rule, and Sir Edwin Andros, a man of excellent private character, but of abominable political principles, was sent over to govern the whole region of country between Chesapeake Bay and the Penobscot River. Andros was one of those narrow-minded, hard-headed persons who can see nothing but the will of their master; who can be more despotic than the despot himself, and whose private virtues seem all the more strange in contrast with their abominable public characters.

The English people had long been outraged in their rights and liberties by their treasonable servants, the Stuart kings. They had passed through a civil war and were suffering from the folly of the reaction brought about by the aristocracy and nobles. They were now getting ready to drive out one king, as they had already beheaded another. Furthermore, they were especially incensed at the buccaneer who had become their sovereign, and was now the ally and tool of Louis XIV., who had driven the Huguenots out of France.

Andros seemed to have no idea but to out-Stuart the Stuarts. In New York he tried hard to set up the state religion of England, and to exploit the notions of his master, James II., in defiance of law; but he soon found that the cosmopolitan population of New York — Dutch, Scottish, Irish, English, Welsh, German, and French — were united against him, as against a common enemy. These law-abiding people began to organize that long course of constitutional resistance to the pretensions and usurpations of Andros and the other English governors, — who were mostly intemperate, immoral, and haters of popular liberty, besides being land speculators of a disreputable sort. The good people in the Dutch Reformed churches, by their tenacity to their religious convictions, by their upholding of popular education, by their refusing in the Assembly to vote for the governor's measures, were especially active in saving freedom in that typical American colony which was destined to become the Empire State.

Andros, in pursuance of the royal ideas which James Stuart was exploiting in England, continued the systematic extinction of charters and local government. He punished the little town of Schenectady, by declaring a blockade and the stopping of its trade for nearly three months. His attempt to crush out the instincts of the liberty-loving colonists, though utterly vain, seemed to the Huguenots in New York wonderfully like the course of Louis XIV., and to the Netherlanders like that of Philip II.

When James II. came to the throne, he determined to take away the charters of Connecticut and

Rhode Island, as his brother Charles II. had already done in the case of Massachusetts, and to unite all New England in one royal province. For violating the Navigation Laws, for welcoming the two judges who are called by English historians "regicides," for opposition to England's political church, for being too republican, Massachusetts was made a province of the crown like New York, and remained so until the Revolutionary War, Andros being the first royal governor.

In order to bring the people of Connecticut directly under his control, Governor Andros, backed by a body of soldiers, went to Hartford to get the charter. The people resolved they would not give this up. Governor Andros discussed the matter with the legislature until it was dark. Then, as tradition avers, the charter was brought in and placed on the table. Suddenly the candles were blown out. When they were lighted again, no charter was seen. Some one, according to the story, had seized the document and hidden it in a hollow of an oak tree near by, which was ever afterwards known as "Charter Oak" and stood till 1856. Nevertheless, Andros declared that charter government in Connecticut was null and void. A marble tablet stands where the old oak tree did, and a piece of one of its boughs, in the form of a bell-yoke, is now in Independence Hall in Philadelphia.

Everything looked dark for freedom, from the Delaware to the Kennebec, and the descendants of men who had known liberty in Great Britain and the Netherlands were discouraged, when suddenly there came a gleam of light from Holland. William III., great-grandson of William the Silent, the pioneer of constitutional and religious freedom, had married into the Stuart family of England. His wife was the daughter of King James II. Having been invited by the leading men of England to come over with his army and take the throne in place of the ruler who had betrayed the nation, William set sail with his Dutch fleet and regiments. Of his fine army of fifteen thousand men, probably half were Huguenots. Landing at Torbay, he marched to London. Soon afterward his wife was made the Queen and he the King of England. From this time forth, to Christians outside the political church, life was less of a burden, though the free churchmen had to study in Holland or Scotland, for English universities were still shut to nonconformists.

Parliament issued that great state paper which marks the revolution of 1688 as the beginning of modern parliamentary government, whereby almost all power is centred in the House of Commons, and Great Britain has become a republic, though still retaining the form of a monarchy. The Declaration of Rights, drawn up chiefly by Lord

Somers, is modelled on the Dutch Declaration of Independence of 1581. Since 1688, English free churchmen have been able by persistent struggle to win their rights. The Puritan revolution in which Charles Stuart was executed as malefactor was justified, and not a few of the ideas and the hopes of Cromwell were carried out. Since 1688, also, many of the modern reforms, which had long existed in Holland, had become a part of English law and custom.

When William III. crossed over to Ireland also, many hundreds of his Dutch and Huguenot soldiers settled down in Ulster. They, with civilians from Holland, introduced new industries and manufactures, the raising of flax, the making of fine textiles, and of that renowned Irish linen which soon brought wealth to the Emerald Isle. Ulster "County" became a garden of intelligence and thrift, and a school for the cultivation of the noblest virtues that adorn humanity. Here were bred the ancestors of possibly ten million Americans and hundreds of men and women who have been leaders in American history.

James II. never regained office in England and his grandson Charles Edward, known in England as "The Young Pretender" and in Scotland as "Bonny Prince Charlie," attempted, in 1744, with a large fleet and French force to invade England, but a storm destroyed both his ships and his plans. In

the next year he landed in Scotland. The High-
landers rose in his favor and won several victories
over the royal troops; but at the battle of Culloden,
April 16, 1746, his army was destroyed and with
it the last hope of the Stuarts, whose line became
extinct in 1807. This battle broke up Gaelic feudalism and the clan system in Scotland. The High-
landers were enlisted as soldiers in the British army,
or scattered all over the world, large numbers coming to America. From this time forth, the bagpipe
was heard and the gay Gaelic dress of tartan plaid
seen in other lands. Armed with virtues nourished
beside the loch, under the granite ben and in the
glens, on moor and turf, and heather and gorse, the
Scotsman went forth to do most nobly the world's
work, and to help build the greatest of republics.

CHAPTER XX.

GOVERNOR LEISLER, THE HUGUENOTS, AND THE ROYAL WARS.

WHEN the people of the colonies heard of the revolution in England, they at once made movements to regain law and freedom. In New York, on May 31, 1689, Jacob Leisler, a German or Huguenot commissioner of the Court of Admiralty, took the fort on Manhattan Island, declared for the Prince of Orange, and planted six cannon within the fort, from which the place was ever afterwards called "The Battery." A committee of safety was formed which invested Leisler with the powers of a governor. When, however, a despatch arrived from the authorities of Great Britain, directed "to such person as, for the time being, takes care for preserving the peace, and administering the laws in his majesty's province in New York," Leisler, considering himself governor, dissolved the committee of safety, and organized the government throughout the whole province. There was. division among the New Yorkers. The minority, being mostly the English aristocracy, were against

Leisler, but the people in great majority were in sympathy with him. It was the old conflict between the few and the many, with " all the people " sure in the end to win.

Louis XIV. of France aided, with his fleet and army, the refugee and pretender James Stuart, to invade Great Britain. This made the Dutch and British once more comrades in arms, in a war against the enemies of law and liberty. The Edict of Nantes, issued by Henry IV. of France, in 1559, which granted religious toleration, was revoked by Louis XIV. in 1685, and the French Christians of the Reformed church were hunted out of France, grandly to the gain of America. Massachusetts, the Carolinas, and New York profited most by getting these people of high character, culture, graces, and abilities. To the French refugees coming to New York, Governor Leisler gave a welcome and made provision for them by purchasing land at New Rochelle. Here, in New York city, at New Paltz, and other places, these excellent people helped build up the noble commonwealth of New York.

The echoes of the strife in Europe were quickly heard in American forests. Soon began the first of several wars, royal rather than popular, which were destined to make New York the tramping and battle ground of armies and the region whence parties of Canadian French and savages should march to ravage the frontier settlements. New England's battles were to be fought mostly by sea.

Jacob Leisler was probably among the very first of far-sighted men to see the necessity of union against the French, who represented the Latin idea of civilization, while the Dutch and British represented the Germanic or modern idea of self-government. To him, the importance of a federation of all the colonies seemed vital. After plainly trying to get other governors to unite with him, Leisler, early in 1690, sent a small fleet against Quebec. From the very first New York was infused with that sentiment for union which she has shown in all political disturbances and wars throughout all her history. Very appropriately, on her soil, was held the first Congress to propose an elaborate plan of union.

As soon as news of the English revolution reached Boston, where Andros lived, the people put their tyrant in prison and restored their self-government, which they maintained until a royal governor was sent over by the new king. Then, of Maine, New Hampshire, and Massachusetts, including Plymouth Colony, was made one royal province.

What we call "King William's War," the beginning of a conquest which was to rage for over seventy years, broke out in 1689. It was only the cis-Atlantic part of a long struggle between Great

Britain and France to settle the ownership of India and North America. In Europe the bloody theatre of the fighting which was to last, with some intervals, until the battle of Waterloo was chiefly in the southern Netherlands, though at first in the Rhine Palatinate. On our continent the contest was to decide the question whether the colonists were to grow up under a Latin or a Germanic ideal of civilization. Usually represented as four distinct wars, the American phase of this prolonged campaign was in reality but one war, which was to end at the fall of Quebec.

Until 1763 the French determination to get hold of America was as strenuous and persistent as the English. Frontenac, a relative of Madame Maintenon, the mistress of Louis XIV., and who had seen service in the Dutch and Italian wars, had been appointed governor-general of Canada in 1672. He built Fort Frontenac where Kingston, Ontario, now stands. He assisted the exploring expeditions of La Salle, Marquette, and Joliet in the Mississippi valley. When, in 1682, the governor was recalled, the colony in Canada almost fell into ruins. In 1689 he was sent back again.

Almost at once the whole continent seemed to feel the magic of Frontenac's iron hand. Within a few months, his sailors had destroyed the English fleet in Hudson's Bay and invaded Newfoundland. His raiding parties ravaged the Iroquois territory

and captured or burned Pemaquid, Casco, Salmon
Falls, and Haverhill in New England and Schenectady in New York. Frontenac's courage and
activity were marvellous. For several years it looked
as if the fallen fortunes of France in America were
to be restored. His method of terrorizing the
whole colonial frontier, from Maine to New Jersey,
was to send out small bands of French and Indians
to surprise and shoot down the settlers in the field
and burn their villages.

In 1690 Haverhill was the frontier town in Massachusetts. The Indians attacked the town and
carried off as captives two women and a boy. On
the way to Canada, while the savages were asleep,
Mrs. Hannah Dustin succeeded in killing her cap-
tors with their own tomahawks and returned to the
settlement with ten scalps. On the 9th of February, 1690, a party of over two hundred French and
Indians surprised Schenectady, New York, at mid-
night. They slaughtered the Connecticut soldiers
in the fort and the Dutch people in the village,
sixty in all, taking nearly as many prisoners. They
then burned the houses and escaped to Canada. In
our day many a "mossy marble" and roadside
memorial tells of the colonial pioneers of the border,
slain at their ploughs or in the field by invisible
gunners, killed in their homes by French or red
men, or "captivated by the Indian salvages."

A hard-drinking Englishman, named Sloughter, was appointed the royal governor of New York. On his arrival, Leisler refused to surrender the fort and government, until convinced that Sloughter was the regularly appointed agent of the king. Those who hated Leisler seized this opportunity of having him and Milborne, his son, imprisoned. After a short and absurd trial, they were condemned, and the governor, when drunk, signed an order of execution. On May 16, 1691, Leisler and Milborne were hanged on the spot east of the Park in New York city, where stands the Tribune building, opposite which are the statues of Benjamin Franklin and Nathan Hale and near which the figure of Leisler may yet come to resurrection in bronze. The outrageous act of the king's agent was disapproved. In 1695, by an act of Parliament, Leisler's name was honored, indemnity was paid to his heirs, and the remains of these victims of judicial murder were honorably buried within the edifice of the Reformed Dutch church. No unprejudiced historian can but honor Leisler, the lover of union, and the champion of the people's rights.

During King William's War, the colonists of Massachusetts sent an expedition, which captured Port Royal and Nova Scotia, then called Acadia. They also made an attack on Quebec, which, how-

ever, was brilliantly repulsed under Frontenac.
Louis XIV. was so much pleased over this event,
that he had a medal struck in honor of the French
victory. Peace was finally made in 1697, by the
envoys of Great Britain, France, Spain, Germany,
and the United Netherlands, who met in the summer palace of the Dutch stadholder at the little
village of Ryswick near The Hague. A grand
partition of the continent of America among three
Powers was temporarily agreed upon.

The British people were not well pleased with
the Peace of Ryswick. They grumbled and declared that the only benefit which they had received, for all their expenditure of blood and money
on the European continent, was the acknowledg-
ment by the French of William III. as King of
England. Yet the British government had spent
very little treasure, and sent but few men to
America, during King William's War, the colonies
having done almost all the fighting.

Such a peace could not be permanent. Five
years later, the strife broke out afresh. This time
it was called in America " Queen Anne's War,"
after Queen Anne of England. It lasted from
1702 to 1713. Deerfield, in Massachusetts, was attacked by red and white Canadians. The sun
rose on a thriving village one morning and on
the next lighted up a level waste of ashes. The

Eastern colonies recaptured Port Royal and named it Annapolis, in honor of the queen. In the attempt, in 1711, to take Quebec, the expedition under Sir Harrenden Walker encountered stormy weather and suffered from the ignorance of the pilots. The ships were wrecked, and over a thousand lives were lost, the whole affair ending in disaster.

In the South the people of the Carolinas were attacked by the Tuscarora Indians, who had evidently been urged on by the Spaniards. In one night, near Roanoke, they massacred a hundred and thirty-seven white settlers and seemed inclined to drive the pale faces entirely off the soil. Governor Craven of South Carolina at once appointed Colonel John Barnwell, an Irishman, to take vengeance on the savages. Gathering a body of six hundred white and several hundred allies, all of them well used to woodcraft, and able to subsist in the forest without provision trains, " Tuscarora John " drove the hostile warriors before him. He compelled them to fight at a disadvantage with men who could stand up behind trees and use all the red men's tricks against themselves. Then besieging them in their fortified castle, Barnwell compelled the braves of this once mighty tribe to surrender. After one thousand of their fighting men had been killed, the shattered remnant of the Tuscarora tribe was compelled to leave the old hunting grounds and to come north into New York. In 1713 they settled in the region of Cayuga Lake, joining the confederacy of the five Iroquois tribes, which were hereafterwards known as the Six Nations.

No other events of importance occurred during this war, which was concluded in 1713, after heavy fighting in the Netherlands, in which the Duke of Marlborough made his great fame. By the Treaty of Utrecht Acadia now became a part of Great Britain and was named Nova Scotia.

CHAPTER XXI.

THE MOHAWK VALLEY AND THE PALATINE GERMANS.

DURING the interval of peace from 1713 to 1744, there was a westward movement of the colonists from the older coast settlements. Pioneers from eastern and central Massachusetts occupied the region of the Berkshire Hills. In Pennsylvania the Palatine Germans settled the region between the Delaware and Lehigh and the Susquehanna. New York west of Schenectady was opened to settlement. In the Mohawk valley, Hendrich Frey from Zurich, Switzerland, had made his home west of the Palatine Bridge before 1700. After 1710, thousands of Germans from the Rhine Palatinate, who had left their fields and vineyards, gladly entered New York as the new land of promise on the Livingston Manor, and, later, by the Schoharie and Mohawk, becoming good Americans.

These Germans were at first very poor, but whether of the Lutheran or of the Reformed churches they were devout God-fearing people of high principle. They were especially tenacious of personal liberty, just as their Teutonic forefathers were. Those who tried to play the Roman Cæsar over them soon found out their folly to their own cost. All know how their tenacity and courage were splendidly shown at the battle of Oriskany, the most bloody and severely contested, and by some thought to be the decisive battle of the Revolution. Not all Americans, however, are familiar with the fact that through the Palatine German, Zenger, the freedom of the press in America was first won.

The fur trade received a tremendous stimulus, when, in 1722, the British flag was unfurled by Governor William Burnett at Oswego, which was the first English outpost on Lake Ontario. Burnett encouraged bold young men from Albany and the valley settlements to penetrate to Niagara and beyond. These sturdy traders were ever alert, whether on water or land. They could either paddle their canoes or carry them from stream to stream. Their outfit of manufactured articles was exchanged for cargoes of peltry.

In 1727 a regular fort was built at Oswego, and then began the development of the American commercial traveller, the prototype of the smart, well-dressed, and brainy "drummer" of to-day. Instead of riding with thousand-mile tickets in express trains and palatial sleeping-cars, having sample bags and trunks, and stopping in comfortable hotels in which to show their wares, these colonial pioneers of trade, full of courage, address, and rich in resources, used the birch-bark canoe and the pack-horse. They carried their hardware, dry-goods, and ornaments out, and their bundles of furs in, so that Albany became the headquarters of that fur trade in America, as London and Amsterdam were in Europe.

It was in 1738, the year that King George III. was born, that Sir William Johnson began his activities as an Indian trader, and aided in the further development of the Mohawk valley, the natural highway to the great West. Lieutenant John Butler, who had been in the ill-fated expedition against Quebec, had already settled with his two sons near the later Johnstown. In 1740 Johnson was appointed head of the Indian department. The Butlers and Johnson were Irishmen, with the wit and abilities of their race. A few years later came the Campbells and other Scotsmen, who settled at Cherry Valley. Johnson continued the work so nobly begun by Arendt Van Curler, the founder of the peace policy with the Iroquois. He learned their language, treated them with justice and kindness, won their friendship, and made them permanent friends of the British.

By the Treaty of Utrecht, it was declared that the Five Nations were subject to the dominion of Great Britain. The English interpreted this to mean that the hereditary territory of the Iroquois and all their conquests westward to the Mississippi River were British property. This the French disputed, and at once there began a struggle for the possession of the Ohio valley. The Virginians opened a road over the Blue Ridge Mountains and petitioned that a fort be built on Lake Erie. New York, Pennsylvania, and Virginia proceeded to strengthen their alliance with the Iroquois by a new covenant at Albany, the ancient place of treaties. For rum, money, and presents, the red men agreed to cede to the English all the lands west and north of Lake Erie.

The French, having been greatly vexed because their trade with the Indians was intercepted at Oswego, now began to think of fortifying Niagara. They also pushed up Lake Champlain, and in 1731 built Fort Carillon at Crown Point. This act alarmed the people of Massachusetts even more than those of New York. The French also tried to lure away the Iroquois from their allegiance to the English; but "the covenant of Corlaer" was not easily broken, and in 1744 the Indians came to Lancaster, Pennsylvania, and again confirmed their former concessions in a new treaty. By this time, the French on both sides of the ocean were irritated and ready to take up arms again in what is known as "King George's War," which lasted from 1744 to 1748.

The greatest event of King George's War was the organization of an expedition in Massachusetts led by Colonel Pepperell of Maine, who, with several thousand farmers and fishermen of New England, captured the great French fortress of Louisburg on Cape Breton Island. This they did with the help of a British fleet under Sir Peter Warren. This victory gave tremendous encouragement to the people of the Eastern colonies.

During these four years the New York people were too busily engaged with their governors in the contest for liberty to pay much attention to the Indians, and so their frontier was opened to the raids of the Canadians, red and white. The king's agent, Clinton, wished to govern without giving account to the Assembly or to the tax-payers, while the people were determined to have a free press, reasonable rights in raising and disbursing taxes, and a voice in directing the policy of the colony. They felt that to win their rights was even more important than repelling savages. The descendants of those who had made the Dutch republic, where " no taxation without consent " was the rule and where resistance to despotic government had been exalted into a principle, were reinforced by all lovers of liberty in New York, whether of Huguenot, Scottish, Irish, Welsh, or German blood. Their steady love of law in opposition to lawless governors, which continued down to the Revolution, showed that New York was leading all the colonies in outgrowing the colonial spirit.

It was these New Yorkers who took the first step which led to separation from the trans-Atlantic country, whose rulers seemed to refuse to learn how colonists ought to be governed, — especially colonists who had been bred in the spirit not of the monarchy and state church of England, but of republican Holland. They did indeed lose, by Indian attacks, the village of Saratoga and some farms and colonists, but they won their freedom against the governors who so steadily misrepresented the spirit of English law.

In November, 1733, John Peter Zenger, who as a boy had come over in the Palatine emigration and learned printing from Bradford in Philadelphia, established *The New York Weekly Journal.* The next year, having criticised the king's foolish representative, Governor Cosby, the latter had his critic thrown into jail. James Alexander Hamilton, of Philadelphia, who had come from Scotland to enjoy more freedom in William Penn's colony, and who first purchased Independence Square for the erection of the State House, in which the Liberty Bell hangs, came on to New York. At his own expense he defended Zenger and secured his acquittal. Thus one of the greatest of all victories in behalf of law and freedom, ever won in this continent, was secured.

In 1747 Governor Clinton, following Cosby's blunder, declined to account to the Assembly for the manner in which he distributed "the money of the crown," *i.e.* the taxes paid by the people of New York. He forbade Parker, the public printer, to publish the address and remonstrance of the Assembly against the executive encroachments of power. Parker, refusing to obey Clinton, stood by the people and the Assembly, and printed the address in which they asserted their rights. On the same day on which, thirty-six years afterwards, the British and Hessians evacuated Manhattan Island, Clinton declared to the representatives of the people of New York that their "grasping for power, with an evident tendency to the weakening of the dependency of the province on Great Britain . . . is of most dangerous example to your neighbors." This was true. The action of New York strongly influenced the other colonies to uphold ancient law and freedom.

Sir William Johnson's activity along the frontier greatly improved matters and prevented the French and Indians from winning further advantages by their marauding parties. In the middle of July, a conference was held at Albany, at which Governor Shirley and the Massachusetts commissioners were present.

CHAPTER XXII.

THE SCOTCH-IRISH EMIGRATION.

THE Pilgrims, the Huguenots, and the Scotch-Irish were alike in one respect. They were doubly colonists. They had had two homes before coming to their third home in America.

Next to England, Scotland and Ireland furnished the larger number of colonists in America, before the Revolutionary War. Where people from the Continent by thousands and Englishmen by myriads, the Scottish and Irish came by hundreds of thousands. At the Revolution they numbered nearly one-half of the population of the thirteen colonies. Without the Scotch-Irish, we should never have had the country that we have now. Not only did they equal in numbers all other nationalities from Europe, but in the solid qualities that make up manhood and citizenship, it is doubtful whether they have had any superiors.

In the early Christian ages, both Scotland and Ireland, but more especially the latter country, performed an important part in Christianizing Europe.

Ireland led all Western countries, both as the seat of Christian light and knowledge and in missionary activities in other countries. The greatest saint of the island, the son of a patrician and deacon named Calipurnius, was not Irish or Romish, nor was his name Patrick. Yet his was a character whom all Christians and good men of every age and creed honor. He was a Catholic Christian, long before the later disputes between Germanic and Latin Christianity divided Christendom, and before the names of Romanist and Protestant were heard of. After his death, his disciples continued his noble work.

The Keltic Irish, who have come so largely into the United States, and mostly in the present century on account of famine and troubles in their own country, have suffered many wrongs and sorrows at the hands of English monarchs, lords, and lawmakers. Before the year 1772, only a comparatively small number of people from the southern countries of the Emerald Isle came to America. The great emigration of three hundred thousand or more people from Ireland before 1750 was from Ulster Province, which has a history which may well be called one of the romances of colonization. This ancient division of Erin has in it nine counties, in which are many hills and bogs and much worthless land, yet good colonists made it one of the fairest and richest portions of the earth, and this within one or two generations.

Queen Elizabeth, like other English sovereigns, had attempted to settle English colonies in Ireland, but without much success. In the time of James Stuart, two noblemen of Ulster rebelled. The king confiscated their estates, giving back the bogs, fens, and poor land to the tenantry, but saving the best soil, about five hundred thousand acres, for Scottish colonists. These came over by the thousands, so that by 1641 fifty per cent of the population of a million and a half people were Scottish people, whose numbers throughout the century were augmented by the persecuted Covenanters from Scotland. Before 1700 there were, besides these Scotch-Irish people and their children, many thousands of English and Welsh people, as well as Huguenots and Dutchmen who had accompanied King William. Thus a mixture of the best races of the world had already begun, forming the new man in history, the Ulsterman, usually called "Scotch-Irish," though more exactly a product of at least five of the races which led in civilization. Introducing improved agriculture and the industries of Holland and France, they made of the wilderness a garden and of Ulster a hive of industry.

Greed and bigotry, however, nearly ruined this wonderful colony, and America again profited by the foolishness and wickedness of England's state-church bigotry and the greed of her avaricious people. The repressive legislation of Parliament destroyed the Irish woollen industry and stopped the looms. This left twenty thousand intelligent artisans out of employment. These, by crossing the Atlantic, began that systematic emigration which brought from Ireland a third of a million of the best sort of colonists to the American shores to find, like the Pilgrims, a third home. Not satisfied with industrial oppression, the British government in 1704 passed a Test Act which, like Queen Elizabeth's laws, was equally severe against Calvinists and Catholics. Most cruelly and brutally was this Test Act enforced by Protestant state churchmen under Queen Anne and the Hanoverian kings.

From this year, 1704, until our Revolution, all classes of people from the north of Ireland, who refused to live under such oppression and bigotry, crossed the ocean to America. Indeed, it was hard to find ships enough to bring them over. In Philadelphia ten or twelve thousand of these splendid builders of a nation would come in a single year. Sometimes two or three ships would arrive in a day. The exodus was unusually great after 1720.

Yet as if the oppressed Irishman had not suffered enough, the system of eviction, which for over a century has cursed Ireland, began only three years before the battle of Lexington. The abominable system of raising the rents and basing the increase on the value of improvements was put into force in 1772. At least thirty thousand people, hating the very name of England and especially of English landlords, left the Emerald Isle, and within two years came to America. Most of these emigrants were not poor bog-trotters or potato-eaters who had lived in hovels, but were industrious, well-educated, thrifty, virtuous people of faith and character. Of this great host, many came to New England as early as 1715, and probably as many as fifty thousand in all. Twice as many entered the Southern colonies, but the greater majority came to Pennsylvania and the middle region, whence, gradually, they scattered into all the colonies. At the breaking out of the Revolutionary War, the colonists from Ireland numbered not very far from one million people, a majority being Covenanters or "Scotch-Irish," that is, Scottish-English-Huguenot-Dutch-Irish, a splendid composite. In all the thirteen colonies, there were, in 1775, not quite three million souls, of which about one-half were south of Mason and Dixon's line, and one-half north of it.

A great volume would be needed to tell the influence and results of this, the largest emigration to America. It was not very romantic for either Great Britain or Ireland, any more than for France or Germany, to lose so large an elect portion of their population; but it is a large element in the romance of the colonization of America. The people of this composite stock were of splendid physical vigor and rich in intellect and character. Their good works are especially seen in education, to say nothing of religion, learning, enterprise, and political genius. Almost all the schools and colleges in the Southern colonies before the Revolution were of their founding, and much the same may be said of the Middle states. In these institutions were trained many of the leaders of the Revolution, — warriors, statesmen, men of foresight and leadership.

I frankly confess that, at the Centennial Exposition at Philadelphia in 1876, nothing, in all that gathering of the world's product of mind and hand, so impressed me as the library of books written by the graduates of Princeton College, which had been first begun by the Scotch-Irish in a log cabin. The majority of the patriots in the Continental armies, outside of the Eastern colonies, were from these people. In Hanover, Middletown, Westmoreland, Fort Pitt, and Chester counties in Pennsylvania, and at Mecklenburg, North Carolina, in 1774 and 1775, they were the first to declare for independence.

Many pages of this book would not suffice to

print the long list of thousands of eminent men from this body of colonists. The names of one-half of the presidents of the United States, of vice-presidents, senators, representatives, cabinet officers, and foreign envoys of the United States by the hundreds; of governors, civil and military officers in the colonies and states, by the thousands; of George Clinton, William Livingston, Thomas McKean, Richard Caswell, Edward Rutledge in the colonies; of fourteen of the fifty-five signers of the Declaration of Independence; of Generals Knox, Sullivan, Stark, Montgomery, Wayne, Howard, Campbell, Morgan, Pickens, Clarke, in the Revolution; of Oliver Hazard and Matthew C. Perry; of heroes on both sides in the Civil War to be counted, as officers by the thousands, as privates by tens of thousands, would be in the list. No romance of colonization could ignore this mighty movement. In all our country's history no fact is more apparent.

CHAPTER XXIII.

WASHINGTON, THE COLONIAL FRONTIERSMAN.

THE dynastic and Indian wars, in which the colonists had been compelled to take part, were as so many terms in a school by which the people were gradually educated into the ideas of union, with common interests, and one language, nationality, and destiny. The first wars, such as the " Pequot " and " King Philip's," or that with the Mohicans or the Tuscaroras, had been those of races, — between the white and the red men. Into the wars with the French, the colonists had been dragged because of European politics and their connections with the mother country, but none of them thus far caused a general movement, or had occupied the attention of *all* the colonies. Nevertheless, there was an increasing community of interests and dangers, of hopes and fears, which brought a good many colonists together to act as brothers in the same cause. Men now began to see that it would be a good thing if all the colonies could act together in unity.

The "old French war," from 1744 to 1748, was

really the war of the "Austrian Succession." Begun in Germany, it was ended in Europe, Asia, and America. The peace, which came without honor, settled nothing regarding the question at issue in America. Indeed, the treaty was so made that it guaranteed another war. This time, beginning in 1755 and lasting until 1763, the strife was to break out first in America, before England and France should be involved. Instead of being the "king's war," it was to be one of the people.

The situation, to one who wanted to see North America governed according to Anglo-Saxon ideas, was a serious one. Although there were twice as many people under English rule between Maine and Florida, as there were Frenchmen in all North America, yet the French possessed the two largest and longest rivers of the continent, — the St. Lawrence with its great lakes and tributaries, and the Mississippi River with its many branches. With only two or three "carries," a canoe, or a fleet of canoes, could move swiftly by water from Quebec to the Gulf of Mexico. Between these two points the French had already built forts, by which they commanded the trade with the Indians. Their situations were so well chosen by the French engineers that, although ramparts and palisades have long since vanished, great cities and centres of trade stand on their sites.

One of the first signs that the English and the colonists were waking up to their danger was the organization of the Ohio Company, for the purpose of planting settlements along the head waters of the Ohio River, in what is now western Pennsylvania. Their grant of land gave them five hundred thousand acres, between the Kanawha and the Monongahela rivers, in southern Pennsylvania and northern West Virginia. This region was then rightly called " the gateway of the West," because it controls the streams and valleys running out from New York and Pennsylvania toward the Mississippi valley. It was in the highest degree of strategic importance.

Lawrence Washington, who had been educated in England, was made the chief manager of the company. Lawrence was the older brother of George. He had served under the British admiral Edward Vernon in the West Indies, taking part in the bombardment of the Spanish ports of Porto Bello and Cartagena. He had brought home with him a Dutch soldier, Jacob Van Braam, who became George Washington's military instructor. He named the estate, left him by his father, Mount Vernon. While occupied in frontier business, Lawrence secured the appointment of his brother George, then only nineteen years old, as assistant adjutant-general of Virginia with rank of major. Then " old Van Braam " and Adjutant Battaile Muse trained the young man to his duties. To Lawrence Washington belongs the honor of the initiation of the settlement of the Great West.

The French did not wait to see, but as soon as they heard, what the English were doing, they sent surveyors, engineers, and soldiers into the Ohio country and began building a new line of forts, from Lake Erie to the junction of the two streams that form the Ohio River. This aroused Governor Dinwiddie, of Virginia, to maintain the English claims, which were based on direct purchase of the Ohio valley from the Iroquois Indians, who, as lords of the soil, having conquered it from the western tribes, had sold it to the whites.

Lawrence Washington died in 1752, but Dinwiddie selected his brother George, whom he ordered to march three hundred miles, with his companions, over the mountains and the rivers and among the Indians, to a place called Venango, to give notice to the French that they were intruders and must be off. At this time Washington was twenty-one years of age, an athletic, well-knit young man, who had received a fair common school education, under his teachers, Messrs. Hobby and Williams. He understood surveying and horsemanship, and had learned woodcraft and, what was most valuable, how to travel and live in the forest. On such journeys he used to wear the usual buckskin costume of the trapper and pioneer. On occasions of ceremony at home, his outer dress consisted of a long-skirted and red cloth coat having plenty of buttons, with dress sword and sash, knee-breeches, silk stockings, and silver-buckled shoes. Besides a long waistcoat with stock, ruffles, and lace cuffs, he put on a cocked hat. On his breast hung the polished brass gorget, such as all officers wore, showing his allegiance to the king.

Two years' instruction under the Dutch officer, Jacob Van Braam, had perfected him in the manual of arms, and given him an insight into tactics and fortification. It is very probable that this veteran military instructor told Washington much about Maurice, Prince of Orange, the great soldier of the republic, who had done wonders with a very small army, who accomplished so much by the spade and earthworks, and who made engineering so large a part of the soldier's profession. It is certain that during all his military life, Washington, the surveyor-boy who became commander-in-chief, relied much on earthworks and engineering, and did as great wonders with his little army as Maurice had done with his.

With only two or three companions, the young assistant adjutant of Virginia, in 1753, made the journey over the mountains and delivered his message to the French commander, but received no satisfactory reply; so that it became evident that military force would have to be used to settle the question of ownership.

From the first, Washington had wisely invested his earnings as surveyor in well-selected Virginia lands. This journey to what was then the almost unknown " far West" laid the broader foundations of Washington's fortune, and he became one of the richest men in the colonies, and able to serve without salary. He bought large areas of the Western territory, which he believed would one day be occupied and made into homes for English-speaking people. Ever afterwards he was interested in the question of opening the West to civilization, by making highways on land and by water, so as to secure easy communication for travellers, and to bring the Western products to the Eastern markets.

Thus what is called the " French and Indian War" was really begun in southwestern Pennsylvania, with Washington as the chief actor. The Ohio Company began building a fort at the junction of the two rivers, but the workmen were driven away by the French, who seized the place and named it Fort Du Quesne, after their naval commander, then governor of Canada, who had fought De Ruyter and the Dutch and Spaniards in the Mediterranean. Washington, now adjutant of the colony and lieutenant-colonel of a Virginia regiment, was sent as the governor's agent with power. In April, 1754, he set out with two companies for Mill Creek, arriving after a three weeks' rough journey. After a skirmish and a siege in Fort Necessity, he surrendered to superior force, and returned home defeated, but with honor.

On reaching Mount Vernon again, the name of Washington was upon every lip. He deserved high honors, but the way in which he was treated shows how foolish the British authorities behaved and how they alienated the Americans from loyalty to the king. It was made a rule that colonial officers, no matter what their rank, should be subordinate to British officers of the same grade. The men who came over from England, and knew next to nothing about fighting Indians in the woods, looked with disdain upon American troops, a folly for which many of them paid dearly.

CHAPTER XXIV.

WARNED and urged by the Iroquois Indians, and spurred on by the necessities and dangers of the situation, which grew more serious every day, a convention of the Northern colonies met at Albany, the ancient place of treaties. Among the delegates were Sir William Johnson and Governor Delancey of New York, King Hendrik, the Mohawk chieftain, Benjamin Franklin of Pennsylvania, and Governor Shirley of Massachusetts. To the minds of the Indians, who were then a powerful political factor in the struggle for America, Albany, as being so near Tawasentha, the scene of Hiawatha's labors, and as "the place of many dead," had much the same associations as Westminster Abbey has to a speaker of the English tongue.

With the example of the Dutch republic, the union of the New England colonies, and the Iroquois Confederacy before them, the colonists wondered why they could not unite together to form, as Jacob Leisler had already proposed in 1690, a federal union. The chief newspaper then published in

the colonies was the *Pennsylvania Gazette*, edited
by Franklin. In this he had published the picture
of a snake cut in ten parts, each part named after
one of the Southern or Middle colonies, New England being the head and neck. Underneath was the
motto, " Unite or die."

The Congress enjoyed a public dinner in the
Albany City Hall, June 19, 1764. There were
twenty-five delegates from nine colonies, all being
represented except New Jersey, the Carolinas, and
Georgia. Whether in personal or representative
dignity, this Congress was the most august assembly which had ever been held in the Western world.
The business opened with a paper from Sir William
Johnson and a speech from King Hendrik. Some
of the colonial delegates must have received new
ideas about the right way to deal with the Indians,
for they saw that the New Yorkers believed the red
man capable of understanding and honor, treating
them in the spirit of the Golden Rule and the Ten
Commandments, rather than according to the laws
of Joshua and Ezra. Arendt Van Curler had taught
the method and set the example. On the fifth day,
a motion was made and carried unanimously, that a
union of all the colonies was absolutely necessary for
their security and defence. On the 9th of July the
Congress voted " that there be a union of His Majesty's several governments on the continent, so that

their councils, treasure, and strength may be employed in due proportion against their common enemy." According to this Albany plan of union, there were to be forty-eight members to meet at Philadelphia under a president-general.

From the meeting of colonial delegates in Albany, after the burning of Schenectady in 1690, the word "Congress" had taken on a new meaning, which is very much like that now employed. Furthermore, the idea of a "continental" policy as distinct from the British, the independent as discriminated from trans-Atlantic ideas, grew. In the common talk of the people the continental man was he who was more and more interested in what all the colonies did in union, and less in what the king's ministers were pleased to propose according to their individual whims or notions. The Albany Congress was a great educator of the American people, who began to think, as Wickliffe had long before done, and the Dutch first, and then the British had required, that the dominion of a king ought to be founded in grace, and manifested in the will and ability to govern in righteousness, rather than rest on mere hereditary right. As might be supposed, King George rejected the Albany plan of union, dreading the very idea, as the beginning of independence, and scouting the idea that the colonies should be represented in Parliament.

The British government, responding to the appeal of Governor Dinwiddie, was now thoroughly aroused, and the plan of a general campaign was elaborated. Major-General Edward Braddock, with a force of two thousand regulars and provincials, was to reduce Fort Du Quesne; Governor Shirley of Massachusetts was to capture Niagara; Sir William Johnson, with his Indian militia, was to seize Crown Point; and the Eastern colonists were to attack Acadia. Thus four expeditions were to be set on foot to crush the French power and to maintain the British hold on North America.

The military history of the colonies during this war belongs properly to the romance of war, and not of colonization. Suffice it to say that Braddock was defeated. At Lake George a battle was fought, which was "a failure disguised by an incidental success." Niagara was captured by Sir William Johnson, Fort Du Quesne was taken in a second campaign, New Brunswick was seized, and Louisburg was retaken. About eight thousand Acadians, French people who would not take the oath of allegiance, were compelled to give up their property and to find refuge elsewhere. This was done so hastily that families were separated and much suffering caused. The pitiful story has been partially told in Longfellow's beautiful poem "Evangeline."

Yet, on the whole, the war was rather feebly conducted, until William Pitt was made British Prime Minister. When he succeeded in infusing other men with his own dauntless spirit, the end was not far off.

One of the great decisive battles of the world took place before Quebec, where Montcalm had gathered his forces. He was confronted by Wolfe, who was a soldier from his youth, had seen service in the Netherlands. After the failures of his predecessors he assured his sovereign that he should take Quebec or die. He had arrived in June, 1759, in command of eight thousand men. In the first attack of July 31, he suffered repulse. So long as Montcalm held the great rocky fortress called the Gibraltar of America, and the French admiral had plenty of ships and boats in the river, it seemed as though Quebec would not fall. Yet Wolfe, though ill, discovered through his glass a ravine up which it seemed possible for a forlorn hope to climb. While the English ships perplexed the French admiral and made a feint of landing further up the stream, Wolfe, at the right turn of the tide, took thirty-six hundred men and dropped down the river, where he was joined by twelve hundred men from Point Levi on the opposite side. Then, by climbing up the ladder-like ledges of the rocky ravine, the British forces reached the summit and formed in battle array in the rear of the French host.

Montcalm thought that the British army was still in front of him when the sun rose upon the plateau above the heights of Abraham. Then he heard firing in front of the town, and was surprised to see the red-coated British army in line of battle. Montcalm hurried forward his regiments, while his opponent led his Louisburg grenadiers in the charge. Wolfe was struck by a bullet and taken to the rear. He died happily when he heard that the French were retreating. Montcalm was also mortally wounded, and was glad to be spared the sight of seeing the lily flag lowered over the last stronghold of France in America.

The French gave up their cause as lost, but Pontiac could not accept cheerfully the change of masters. He had long been the ally of the French and was perhaps present at Braddock's defeat. Becoming chief of three large tribes, he organized a conspiracy among all the Indians between the Ottawa and the lower Mississippi. In May, 1763, these confederated red men raised the war-whoop and rushed out on the war-path. Eight of the British garrisons, between Pittsburg and Mackinaw, were destroyed or dispersed on the same day, and the whole frontier was ravaged.

The attack on Detroit, which Pontiac led in person, failed because love was stronger than death. A young Indian girl betrayed the plot to the com-

mander of the fort. It was a new thing for an
Indian to lay siege to a fort, but Pontiac did so,
beleaguering Detroit five months, from the middle
of May to the middle of October. He kept up his
force with food received from the Canadian settlers,
whom he paid with promissory notes written on
birch bark and which he afterwards redeemed. The
scattered war continued for years, but this last
attempt made by many confederated tribes to expel
the white man and to reconquer their hunting-
grounds failed hopelessly.

During all this time the six Iroquois nations remained faithful to the covenant of Corlaer. The
Delawares and Shawnees had got possession of
rifles, which enabled them to carry less ammunition
and move more alertly than when armed with muskets only. The Iroquois were sent out against
them by Sir William Johnson, who traded in scalps
and thus set a bad example to the British government and Continental Congress, in the policy of
employing the Indians in war against white men.

One of the largest conventions of red men ever
held on the continent gathered at Niagara on July 8,
1764, at the call of Sir William Johnson. From
Dakota to Hudson's Bay, and from Maine to
Kentucky, the Indians who were favorable to the
English cause gathered "to brighten the silver
chain of friendship" and with smoking calumet,

shining wampum, and buried tomahawk to swear allegiance to "Kora Kowa,"— the great Van Curler, as the Indians call the sovereign of Great Britain. Hundreds of white captives were given up to their homes and relatives. Johnson's agent went further westward, and Pontiac made overtures of peace. At Detroit on August 17, the Indians, who had lately been in arms, "opened the path of the English from the rising to the setting sun," burying the war hatchet, smoking the calumet, and planting the tree of peace.

Pontiac himself met Johnson at Oswego, July 23. Amid every possible accessory of impressive display and ceremony, besides the sacred tokens of friendship and the sacramental wampum, promises of peace were exchanged. Then Pontiac and his braves moved out in their canoes over Lake Ontario to the west and to obscurity. Henceforth the way of civilization was cleared, and the march of the white men to the Pacific began.

In October, 1768, another convention of Indians was held at Fort Stanwix, now Rome, New York, over three thousand red men being present. For fifty thousand pounds sterling, plenty of rum, and the due exchange of speeches and wampum, the suzerain tribes of the Six Nations, with their allies and vassals, sold outright to the king the vast territory now occupied by Kentucky, western Virginia, and western Pennsylvania. The next year Daniel Boone led from the southern Atlantic coast that great emigration of white men which resulted in the winning of the West. Latin civilization, except as it could be modified by the Germanic-American spirit, had left the whole continent north of Mexico forever.

CHAPTER XXV.

LAWFUL RESISTANCE TO UNLAWFUL TAXATION.

THE French and Indian wars had brought together in comradeship from the various colonies large bodies of men, who had learned much from one another. These, by their experiences, were now inspired to further enterprise. Thousands of brave men had been trained in the use of arms in war. When, as often happened, they saw the regular soldiers of Europe turn and fly, while colonial riflemen stood up and faced the enemy, it took away all fear of "the king's troops" and educated the colonists for the War of Independence.

Furthermore, when the French were no longer a power, the colonists felt less the need of protection from the British government. The Indians, though still a great danger, became of almost no political importance. Practically all hostile forces had been cleared from the region east of the Mississippi. The Alleghany Mountains were no longer a barrier. With such a state of mind and in such a situation, the very highest wisdom in the government at London was needed to rule wisely the American colonies.

It usually happens as between people in the old home land and those in the colonies, that the latter know much more about the people in the mother country than these do about the colonists. To-day, in the United States, the Western people are better acquainted with the Eastern people and affairs than the latter are with the former. The newer people hold tenaciously the old history and traditions, even if they do not follow the latest fashions. The surviving soldiers of the large British armies in America, on returning to Great Britain, told about the land in which there were thriving towns and villages, with churches, colleges and schools, printing presses and newspapers, and rich farms. Popular literature in the old country made English America better known, but it must be said that it came like a surprise to the majority of British people to learn about these colonies, with their governments that raised armies and had navies and that voted large sums of money for carrying on the war. Experiences with Indians profoundly affected the British imagination, which was later fed and stimulated by travellers. Cooper's novels have made most British folks, especially the aristocratic and uncritical, think that red men in feathers, war-paint, fringed buckskin, and moccasins are even yet quite common in the Atlantic coast cities.

It had cost an enormous amount of money to

carry on the war against the French in America, and the taxes laid upon the people to pay the interest on the debt was very heavy. It was during the reign of the Stuarts that Parliament had gained this power of taxing the people and also of dictating to the king. Charles I. and II. and James I. and II. had vainly tried to raise revenue without the aid of the people's representatives. In the struggle between the people and their rulers, the monarch had to give up his powers, so that the power of the chief servant of the people, who sits on the throne to-day, is almost nothing. The queen makes a good and obedient figure-head and Great Britain is practically a republic.

Finding great difficulty in providing the revenue necessary to pay interest on the war debt, the Parliament of King George III. began to think of taxing the colonists in America. So William Pitt arranged a system, borrowed largely from that in use in the republic of the United Netherlands when fighting for independence against Spain from 1568 to 1648. The Dutch had been able to pay their way during eighty years of war by taxing food and drink, windows and chimneys, and almost everything bought, sold, or used. They cheerfully paid their taxes and had almost no war debt, when they had ended their long struggle. This was because they were well represented and voted the budget themselves.

In America, too, in the colonial Assemblies where the people through their own representatives ordered the taxes which they were to pay, they cheerfully voted enormous sums. When they were allowed to say what the salaries of the king's officers should be, they gladly paid these also. When, however, these salaries were fixed in England, or by the governors and judges themselves, without regard to the wish of the colony's representatives, there was continual trouble between the people and their rulers.

The British government determined not only to tax the colonists, but also to enforce the provisions of the Navigation Act. This forbade the colonists to trade with any country except Great Britain. These laws concerning shipping had been made a century before, with the idea of ruining Dutch trade and getting possession of the carrying business on the ocean. For a long time the Navigation Act had not been enforced in the colonies. Colonial fortunes had been made by trading in the West Indies, by sending lumber and fish and getting in return molasses, sugar, and Spanish milled dollars.

When King George III., of that Hanoverian line which showed how many foreign dynasties have ruled England, came to the throne, he, like a conceited young man, was inclined to over-govern.

He vigorously seconded the determination of Parliament to tax the colonies. British ships were sent to the American coast to stop the trade with the West Indies and with Europe. Almost all the tea drunk in the colonies had been smuggled from Holland, and much lucrative trade had long been driven with the Spanish, French, and Dutch West Indies.

The royal officers enforced this law with sudden and great severity. Under what were called Writs of Assistance, they entered the colonists' houses at all hours of the day and night, searching from top to bottom, without regard to the owner's convenience. Nearly all laws can be used as engines of personal spite. This one gave the king's officers and their adherents fine opportunities of wreaking their malice against persons whom they did not like. Thus the import trade of the colonists was nearly ruined. The spirit of the whole policy was exactly that which had broken up the industries of Ireland and compelled thousands of Ulstermen to emigrate to America to save themselves from starvation.

In England certain of the measures of taxation resorted to were very unpopular, especially the tax on windows. In old parts of London, one may still find houses in which windows were bricked up, in order to avoid paying the tax on light. Those who supported George III. in his arbitrary measures not a few of whom were notorious jobbers and speculators, were called "the king's friends." There were also a great many well-wishers of the colonies, some of them in the Parliament, like William Pitt and Edmund Burke, and some outside, like the Rev. Dr. Price. This Unitarian clergyman wrote pamphlets of great vigor, showing keen knowledge of finance and of the principles of liberty. He denounced the wicked schemes and robber-like plans of "the moneyed friends of the government." He declared England to be a stepmother rather than a true parent, and argued that even though most of the colonists were of British descent, this fact conferred no more right upon Great Britain to lay taxes than upon Germany to tax Englishmen because the first historic settlers of England were Germanic tribes. Dr. Price's pamphlets were circulated by the tens of thousands in Great Britain. They were also translated into Dutch by the statesman Van der Capellen, who throughout remained a firm friend of the American cause.

Against the protest of those who understood the American spirit and the principles of civil liberty best, Parliament, which was then, in the main, a very corrupt body of politicians, passed the Stamp Act in 1765. This decreed that all important papers used in legal or business matters, all printed matter, pamphlets, and newspapers were to have stamps put on them, which cost from half a penny to ten pounds. Without the stamps, manuscript or print was illegal.

The Stamp Act was a tremendous stimulant to political discussion. Under its menace, there broke out a war of pamphlets written for and against the measure, but chiefly in opposition. The pulpit was also arrayed against the scheme. One clergyman, Jonathan Mayhew, ridiculed the saintship and martyrdom of Charles I., and asserted the right of the people to disown and resist bad rulers, as Englishmen had done in the previous century. In his last message to James Otis, Mayhew pleaded for a permanent union of the colonies as a defence against evils to come. In Boston Faneuil Hall, built and presented to the city by a Huguenot and called " the old cradle of liberty," after the hall in Utrecht, where the Dutch formed their Union of States, a town meeting was held and in it Samuel Adams denounced the act in fiery eloquence. In London, Benjamin Franklin protested against it. Yet, in spite of all remonstrances, the law was passed. Then royal officers were sent over into all the large towns with a supply of stamps.

There were riots in Boston, and an organization called the Sons of Liberty, which met under a pine tree, tore down the building where the stamps were to be sold, and hanged and burned an effigy of the royal officer who was to sell them. James Otis reaffirmed the principle that taxation without representation was tyranny. In the Virginia Assembly, Patrick Henry spoke so vigorously against the measure and so great was the opposition in other colonies, that the men appointed to sell the stamps were frightened out of their business and the act was not enforced. Nine of the colonies sent delegates to New York and a congress was held, setting forth the ancient Dutch doctrine that the right to tax men belonged to their representatives alone. Yet there was nowhere any objection to pay taxes.

When news of these proceedings in America reached England, Parliament repealed the Stamp Act. Yet, as the objection of the colonists was not to the tax, but to the way in which it was levied and collected, this repeal did not bring satisfaction or allay suspicion. Parliament still foolishly professed the right to tax the colonies. So the next year another act was passed. This imposed duties on imports, such as tea, glass, paint, and paper. To enforce this legislation, agents were to live in the seacoast towns where the British naval officers could protect them. In 1768 General Gage, who had been with Braddock, was sent over with two regiments of soldiers. These soldiers, as well as the royal governors, judges, and other officers, were to be paid with the money raised by the new scheme of taxation projected under the Stamp Act. All the king's servants were to be made independent of the people. This meant an increase of royal power and the decrease of the power of the people, whose right of voting taxes, inherited first from their Germanic and then from their British ancestry, was to be taken away.

The struggle for ancient rights and privileges which now began was to last, in peace and war, for nearly a quarter of a century. The people of the colonies agreed with one another not to buy, sell, or use any of the articles which were taxed. Those who supported the king were called Tories, while the Continentals, or Americans, were called Whigs. Among the former were fine families and individuals of high social and moral character, as well as some rascals and traitors, while among the latter were rough characters; yet the American patriots had most of the right on their side. Not a little bitterness, which in some cases broke out into violence, existed between the adherents of ancient right and law and the loyalists.

CHAPTER XXVI.

GOLDEN HILL, ALAMANCE, AND THE BOSTON MASSACRE.

THE people of New York were especially forward in resisting the arbitrary measures of king and Parliament; for, in addition to the spirit inherited from their own Dutch fathers who had so long battled for liberty, the Germans were irritated at the attempts made directly and indirectly to force the church of England upon them. In the Mohawk valley and on Golden Hill, on Manhattan Island, they erected liberty poles, where affrays took place between the Whigs and Tories. The soldiers cut down and sawed up the liberty pole. On January 18, 1770, on Golden Hill, of which Gold Street is still a remembrance, a fight ensued in which blood was shed, — the first in the Revolution. One man, a sailor, died from his wounds. The reërected liberty pole remained until the British occupation of New York in 1776. A bronze tablet in the Post Office commemorates the fact. Liberty poles were the survival in history of the ancient forest trees, under which the Teutonic tribes assembled in council for war, or to defend their rights.

The first blood shed in the open field by the cannon and musketry of royal soldiers was in the state of North Carolina, where the people were divided in opinion. The admirers and adherents of the British governor William Tryon were mostly on one side, and the friends of righteousness and the people were nearly all on the other. Tryon, an Irishman, had married a relative of the British secretary of state for the colonies, and came over in 1764. At Newbern or New Berne, which had been settled and named by Swiss emigrants in 1710, Tryon, at the expense of the colony, built a magnificent residence. He carried out his notions with such extravagance and rigor that the people became exasperated and formed themselves into an organization to secure justice and better government. These men, mostly Scotch-Irish, were called Regulators. When they took up arms to redress their wrongs, Tryon marched against them with infantry, cavalry, and artillery in large force. At Alamance, on the 15th of May, 1771, he attacked the petitioners when they were unprepared. With his well-served cannon, handled by sailors, and his superior force, he scattered the Regulators and crushed the whole movement with great barbarity, hanging a large number of them.

Tryon's policy so pleased his superiors in Europe that "Bloody Billy," as the colonists called him, was transferred to New York, where the spirit of the people had always held in check the arrogance of the royal governors. Tryon, who was expected to put down the threatening symptoms of dissatisfaction, began, as usual with New York's British governors, to engage first in large land speculations. The region in and about the Mohawk valley, from which at least six counties have since been formed, was named Tryon County. With the aid of his handsome wife and daughters, who had great social influence on Manhattan Island, and by his alertness and energy, Tryon was able to retard the patriot movement in New York.

In front of the State House at Boston, the British soldiers fired upon those who were irritating them by calling them "lobsters," on account of their red coats, and by bandying other epithets. Three men were killed, including Crispus Attucks, a mulatto slave. The blood crimsoning the white snow was never forgotten by the Boston people, and the exact spot is still marked by a circular arrangement of the stones in the granite pavement. The soldiers were defended by James Otis and John Quincy. They were all acquitted except two, who were publicly branded for manslaughter. In Rhode Island the people seized the British vessel, the

Gaspée, by surprise and burned her. The conflict in the colonial Assemblies between the representatives of the people and the royal governors became more intensely bitter.

With strange and fatuous refusal to see the principle involved, Parliament attempted to soothe the American feeling by removing all the taxes except that on tea. Yet the principle was the same for a small tax as for a large one. The colonies knew Dutch and English history too well to allow any tax to be extorted from men who could not themselves vote on the expenditures, or be represented in the voting of the expenses of government.

China furnished the magic leaf which dissolved the bond between the mother country and her grown-up child. Parliament in 1773 allowed tea to be brought to America and sold as cheaply as in England, while the tax was really, but not apparently, to be paid. Yet all this foolish legislation was but hammering or grinding the wedge to a thinner edge, in order to drive it in all the more heavily when once inserted, and the Americans knew it.

When the tea-ships which came from Amoy, China,—where the local pronunciation of the Chinese word *cha* is, as we have received and pronounce it, "tea,"—the people of New York, Pennsylvania, and North Carolina would not allow the chests to be landed, but sent them back. In

Maryland the owner of the tea-ship *Peggy Stewart* set fire to the vessel with his own hand and burned it up. In one or two other seaports the tea, though put ashore, was unbought and allowed to spoil through dampness. In Boston the citizens refused to permit the chests to be taken off the ships, but the royal officers detained the vessels in the harbor, so that on the twentieth day, according to rule, they could be unloaded by the custom-house authorities. On the evening before, a party of men disguised as Mohawk Indians boarded the tea-ships, opened the hatches, and tumbled the Chinese herb out in the water.

Parliament retaliated for the Boston Tea Party's doings by passing acts which shut the port, stopped the city's trade, and changed the government of Massachusetts so as to destroy all popular power. Parliament also united the country north of the Ohio and east of the Mississippi into one dominion, so as to prevent Americans from settling in the conquered territory and in order to conciliate the French colonists and get their aid, if possible, in case of war. American offenders were to be brought to England for trial. In other words, no justice could be obtained on this side of the Atlantic.

After law had been thus trampled on by a government controlled by unscrupulous money-makers, neither order nor freedom was safe. The people had to look on while Massachusetts was handed over to the rule of General Gage and his soldiers. Yet, since all the colonies sympathized with the Bay State, the people now took another step forward. Public opinion now declared that not only taxation, but legislation without representation, must be resisted and, if necessary, by force. In a word, the glorious precedent of the law-abiding Dutchmen in the federal republic founded by the German prince, William of Nassau, the apostle of toleration, was followed by our fathers.

Americans, who have been foolishly taught to "hate the British," ought never to forget that Parliament at this time represented landed property rather than the people, and that King George III. was narrow in mind, sluggish in thought, obstinate, and reactionary in principle. Once bent on a course of action, he could not be easily checked. The war against the American colonies was so unpopular in Great Britain, that even the big bounties offered failed to attract volunteers into the army to do the "King's dirty work" of fighting the colonists, who were standing on their rights. The British people have long ago acknowledged the folly of their rulers, and we ought to know this and honor them for it.

CHAPTER XXVII.

"I WILL MAINTAIN."

THE colonial Assemblies all passed resolutions condemning Parliament so severely, that in nearly every case the governors dissolved them. Several of the colonies were thus left without any real governor. Connecticut was the only colony in which both governor and people formed a unit in resisting revolution from without. In this Puritan democratic commonwealth, "Brother Jonathan" Trumbull was the efficient chief magistrate.

A call was made for another Congress, which met in 1774 at Philadelphia, in the pretty little building called Carpenter's Hall. This was the first "Continental" Congress, because made up of delegates from all the thirteen colonies on the continent. They resolved not to buy, sell, or use English goods, and to support Massachusetts in her struggle. In the colonies, since the people and the royal governors were at strife, nobody knew whom to obey. Committees of safety and correspondence were therefore formed, and these began to collect powder and ball, provisions and military supplies.

They made themselves ready to maintain their rights should the King of Great Britain imitate Philip II. of Spain, by sending his own troops and foreign mercenaries to support usurpation, and force the colonists to pay taxes which they never voted. The motto of William the Silent, " I will maintain," now became that of thousands of men in the Middle colonies, who reëchoed their ancestral watchword.

As the largest British force was in the Bay State, it seemed probable that the outbreak must be there first. So the people of Massachusetts enrolled twelve thousand volunteers, a third of whom were minutemen. These were ready to leave their work and go to fight at a moment's notice. When General Gage received certain information that powder and ball, guns and camp equipage, had been collected at Concord, twenty miles from Boston, he ordered eight hundred men to march out to destroy them. Tryon, in North Carolina, had set him an example and precedent of success, which he was quick to follow.

Now came the question to the people of Massachusetts as to what should be done. If they permitted the destruction of their property, then their conduct would mean that they were submissive to the acts of Parliament. If they resisted by force, it would mean war, but war with whom? Not against the king, for he was their sovereign and in theory all law centred in him and they were his subjects. According to ancient English law, the townsman has a right to go up and down "the king's highway" without molestation, provided he conducts himself peaceably. If townsmen should be met and hindered by the king's troops while on the highway, and the king's troops should fire upon them and injure them, then the townsmen would be innocent. The king's troops would be the aggressors, and whoever ordered them to fire would be guilty and responsible.

In theory, then, and exactly as next day they made affidavit, the king's subjects stood peaceably in the king's highway, when, on April 19, just before daybreak, sixty half-armed "minutemen" were ranged on the village green at Lexington. Captain Parker, their leader, addressed them as freemen standing for right and law, saying, "Men, stand your ground; don't fire unless fired upon, but if they mean war, let it begin here." Major Pitcairn, coming up the road with his redcoats, called the townsmen "rebels," and ordered them to disperse. The law-abiding men of Lexington stood their ground. Knowing their rights, they dared to maintain them.

The violator of English law, Major Pitcairn, discharged his pistols and ordered his men to fire.

The volley stretched seven or eight men, citizens protecting their homes and rights, dead upon the green. War was definitely begun. Revolution had been introduced from without by the act of agents of the king. Henceforth "the British" and "the Americans" were to be two different peoples, even though legal fictions might for a while remain and many good men hope and pray for union.

The British officers expected to be able to arrest two prominent men whom they called rebels. One was named John Hancock, a wealthy merchant of Boston who was at the head of the provisional government. The other was Samuel Adams, who had been very active in organizing committees of safety and correspondence and who had kept up the agitation against parliamentary and royal usurpation. The British failed. The country had been alarmed by Paul Revere, a patriot living in Boston, who, like the Faneuils, Bowdoins, Chardons, Brimmers, and other New Englanders, came of that splendid Huguenot stock which has helped to make the Boston of to-day so lovely.

Leaving Lexington, the British troops moved on to Concord, destroying the military stores by scattering the powder, throwing the cannon-balls into the wells, and breaking up the wooden spoons. On returning, at Concord bridge they met the "embattled farmers." Both parties joined in war upon each other, and the Concord men "fired the shot heard round the world." The Americans remained in possession of the bridge, and the regulars began their retreat to Boston. Now, from all over the country rushed the minutemen with powder horn, bullet pouches, and muskets. From behind stone walls, trees, and bushes they fired upon those they deemed invaders and abettors of wrong. There were scores of little skirmishes at the spots marked to-day with inscribed stones.

The British soldier is not a coward. The men in red coats fought bravely, yet the retreat grew faster and faster. The whole force might have been annihilated, except that Lord Percy met the survivors at Lexington with reinforcements. They had artillery by which to keep the Americans at a distance, yet before they got back to Boston probably three hundred of the British infantry were killed or wounded.

General Gage's army was now shut up in Boston, for the militia, arriving daily from New Hampshire and Connecticut, as well as from Massachusetts, surrounded the city and kept it in a state of siege.

According to the prevalent fictions of law, the Americans had fought their battles in the name of King George against the attempt of Parliament to govern them illegally. There was still no definite idea of separation from the mother country. The royal officers, governors, judges, tax-collectors, etc., fled and took refuge among the British garrisons or on ships of war. The colonial governments were broken up, but provincial congresses carried on political business and maintained order.

The second Continental Congress, which met in Philadelphia, was made up of the ablest men from the colonies. Some of these were John Adams, Samuel Adams, and John Hancock of Massachusetts; John Jay of New York; Robert Morris and Benjamin Franklin from Pennsylvania; Patrick Henry, Thomas Jefferson, and George Washington from Virginia. These were specimens of manhood grown in the colonies, and besides these were many more men in the prime of life and of distinguished ability, well read in the precedents of Dutch law and independence, in More and Harrington, in the literature of the English commonwealth, and the Revolution of 1688, as well as in the ancient law of England and the classic and Biblical story of the rise and development of nations.

This Congress declared the militia gathered around Boston to be a Continental army, and appointed Washington commander-in-chief. Decision was also made, by the act of December 22, 1775, to begin a navy, and soon the shipyards at Kensington had the keels laid of war-vessels, which were built by the "free Quaker" brothers, Manuel

and Jehu Eyre, afterwards officers in the Continental army. These ships were named by John
Adams, after three Italians, the *Columbus, Cabot,*
and *Andrea Doria;* the Saxon *King Alfred;* and
in reliance upon Divine favor, *Providence.* Thus
the initial ships of our gallant navy recalled appropriately the names of the two navigators who began the romance of discovery in America; the ruler
around whom our noblest ancestral traditions cling;
the high-minded Italian, generous and just, who,
even after conquering the city of Genoa, allowed
the people to maintain a republic and to make their
own laws; and that Divine government wherein
even a sparrow's fall is not too minute to be noted.

To begin armed resistance against Parliament, in
the name of King George of Great Britain, was to
do exactly what the Dutch did when they made
war, in the name of Philip II., King of Spain
and Count of Holland, against the Duke of Alva
and other servants of the Spanish monarch. It
was exactly what Cromwell and the parliamentary
party did during the English Civil War, when they
issued commissions in the name of the very king,
Charles II., against whom they were fighting. It
is practically the same theory of law, when it is
understood that one cannot begin suit against the
state, or sovereign power, but only against the
servants of the state.

Ticonderoga and Crown Point were full of munitions of war. In Vermont, Ethan Allen, a Connecticut man, assisted by the Dutch officer Colonel
Bernard Romans, laid a plan to capture the forts.
In the employ of British government, this European engineer had explored and surveyed Florida,
but had resigned his commission and taken up the
American cause. Surprising the sentinels, Allen
rushed into the British commander's room at Ticonderoga and demanded the surrender of the fortress.
This was quickly granted. Within twenty-four
hours, Crown Point was also taken. Cannon, arms,
lead, and powder were transported, on sledges and
otherwise, to Boston, where they were most needed.
For permanent supplies, the Americans relied upon
the captures made by privateers. Until 1780, they
obtained in best quality and greatest quantity
what the army most needed from the Dutch at
St. Eustatius Island in the West Indies. Most of
the " hardware " and "grain," that is, cannon and
powder, with arms and clothing, were made in England and sold by English merchants to Hollanders,
who sent them to America to be exchanged for
tobacco, and the French and Dutch silver and gold
borrowed by Congress.

Washington set out for Cambridge, but before
he arrived the Americans seized Bunker Hill, in
order to build a redoubt by which they could mount

cannon and fire into Boston. They went still nearer and fortified Breed's Hill, where now the battle monument stands. The village of Charlestown lay at the foot of the hill on the edge of the water. At that time Boston was situated on a little peninsula, most of it north and east of the State House on Beacon Hill. All around was water except the narrow neck which united the city to the mainland where Roxbury and Dorchester lay.

When Gage the next morning saw what was being done, he ordered the British ships — some of them lying where is now the solid ground of Commonwealth Avenue — to go near and bombard the Americans. He sent three thousand men in boats, who embarked where the Providence station and the Public Gardens are to-day, and they landed in Charlestown at the foot of the hill. They first ate their lunch leisurely and comfortably before the eyes of the hungry and tired patriots, who looked at them from behind their rude earthworks. The British troops then got ready to advance, as they supposed, to easy victory. They were not even sure whether or not "the Yankees would fight." The Americans were commanded by Colonel Prescott, aided by General Putnam and General Warren, and numbered fifteen hundred men. Instead of bushwhacking, skirmishing, and firing from behind trees and walls, this was to be a battle in force. The ever-brave British soldier, with his bull-dog courage and tenacity, was not likely to give up easily.

The result showed not only that the Yankees would fight, but that they were able to control themselves and hold their fire until they could see the whites of their enemies' eyes and count the fifth button on each red coat. Then a sheet of flame broke from the breastworks. The British ranks were broken ; their breast buttons were towards Boston, and their backs towards the redoubt.

At the foot of the hill, the brave men were re-formed. Again they charged, only to be once more driven back. At the third onset, having galled the Americans on the flanks by means of their artillery, the British were successful and entered the redoubt. The colonials having no more bullets or powder, and unable to keep up the hand-to-hand fight, retreated slowly over toward Cambridge. The British losses were one thousand and fifty-four, the American four hundred and forty-nine. Charlestown village was burned and General Warren killed. Prescott wished to recapture the hill, and declared that if he had had three regiments with bayonets he could do so; but no attempts were made to drive out the garrison, who with true British pluck, as at Lexington and Concord, had persevered, accomplishing what they had set out to do. One incident will show how little thought there was of separating from Great Britain. When General Putnam's regiment in Connecticut was drawn up in line on Cambridge Common, before going into battle, Chaplain Abiel Leonard offered prayer to Almighty God. This is part of his petition : —

"And grant, O Lord, that the inhabitants of Great Britain may arise and vindicate their liberties; and that a glorious reunion may take place between them and Thy people in this land founded upon the principles of liberty and righteousness; that the Britons and the Americans may rejoice in the king as the minister of God to both for good."

Even six months after the battle of Bunker Hill, Philip Freneau, the Huguenot poet of New York, wrote a poem of which the closing stanza was : —

> "Long may Britannia rule our hearts again,
> Rule as she ruled in George the Second's reign.
> May ages hence her growing grandeur see,
> And she be glorious, but ourselves as free."

In fact, the American Revolution, like the Dutch War of Independence, was not begun to obtain utter separation, but to maintain charter rights. Americans as English subjects, whether by descent or under law, vindicated their birthright which the British government wickedly denied them.

CHAPTER XXVIII.

WASHINGTON arrived in Cambridge early in June, 1775. He found an agglomeration of about fifteen thousand men, armed with all sorts of guns and weapons. They were raw militia, poorly clothed and not very willing to submit to military discipline. There was no uniformity in dress. Most of the men wore common tow hunting-shirts, usually dyed brown. The officers, who could afford a suit, wore blue cloth with buff trimmings, which afterwards became the uniform of the Continentals or regular American troops. Washington worked very hard to organize something like an army.

When on this side of the Atlantic it became perfectly certain that King George III. was entirely on the side of Parliament and joined with them in injustice, the desire grew stronger for separation and freedom. New colonial governments had been formed after the king's governors and judges had run away. The people now felt that the colonies were true states and able to take care of themselves.

288

When, on January 1, 1776, the king's proclamation was read in the American camp and it was found that, instead of listening to their humble and loyal petition for justice, he had called them "rebels" and tried to hire Russian and Dutch soldiers to subdue them, and, failing in that, had secured nearly thirty thousand Hessians to do his work, the Americans saw there was no hope of reconciliation.

There was no regular flag, but rather a variety of emblems, such as the pine tree of Massachusetts and the grape vine of Connecticut. As almost all the military words for arms, command, or discipline, such as "tattoo," "tug of war," "forlorn hope," "body-guard," "knapsack," "haversack," and "flag," were of Dutch origin, borrowed or corrupted, from the days when Irish, Scotch, Welsh, and Englishmen fought shoulder to shoulder for freedom in the Netherlands, so also the union flag of the united colonies was like that of the old Dutch naval flag of red and white stripes, one for each colony, with the double cross of St. George and St. Andrew to represent Great Britain. On January 1, 1776, this union flag was raised over the American entrenchments and saluted with thirteen guns. The "stars and stripes" were unknown until long after the Declaration of Independence.

Washington held this army together during the winter, when, as Congress learned that the Canadian British were preparing to march down from northern New York, General Montgomery was sent to take Quebec. Marching by the Lake Champlain way, he captured Montreal. Benedict Arnold, of Connecticut, selected a route, of which Sir William Johnson had told him, through the Kennebec valley and the forests of Maine. His men suffered terribly, and many deserted. Arnold and Montgomery joined forces, and in December they tried to storm Quebec. Montgomery was killed, Arnold was badly wounded, and the Americans were soon driven out of the province. Thus Washington's plan of getting the Canadians to join with the other colonies failed, and Canada, with its mixed French and British people, remained a province of the crown, to which the refugees, Tories and Loyalists, could fly.

Early in the spring Washington seized Dorchester Heights, and had them fortified before General Gage could prevent him. This compelled the evacuation of the city. On the 17th of March, the British troops, with many Tories and Loyalists, sailed away to Halifax. Then Washington and the Continentals entered the city in triumph.

All this time the colonists were fighting in the name of British law and freedom against the illegal claims of Parliament. As the king was a representative of all law and history, they had risen in armed resistance against his servants, but in his name.

In England thousands of persons and many able men believed that the Americans were true to law, and that in fighting for the right of taxation by their own Assemblies, they were doing just what Englishmen had done twice before under the Stuarts. The Continental Congress in issuing their declaration of rights October 14, 1774, wrote, that since they "cannot be properly represented in the British Parliament, they are entitled to a free and exclusive power of legislation in their several provincial legislatures." They petitioned the king October 26, 1774, addressing him as "the loving father" of his "whole people," and beseeching him to hear their complaints and redress their wrongs.

When, however, Parliament heard of the siege of Boston, there was an angry feeling in Great Britain, and the Americans were declared rebels. The government at London made application to Queen Catherine at St. Petersburg for the hire of twenty thousand Russian soldiers to fight the Americans, but the great sovereign of the Russians refused to have one of her soldiers fight for King George against the colonists. Thus began the first of many kindnesses which have always made Americans feel grateful and friendly to Russia.

Then King George applied to the republic of the United Netherlands for Dutch troops, but the Netherlanders, being republicans, sympathized with the Americans and refused a single man. On the contrary, Dutch officers crossed the ocean to serve in the American cause. The Dutch saw that exactly as their own ancestors did, so the Americans were doing in resisting injustice and wicked taxation. All through the Revolutionary War, the Dutch sympathies were very warm in behalf of our fathers. A body of Scotch troops, forming the Scotch Brigade, who had long served the Dutch republic, was required by King George, who sent an autograph letter to his relative, the stadholder, requesting their return to England. The Prince of Orange at this time was William V., who, for aping the ways of British monarchs in a republic, was later driven out of the country, as James II. had been out of England. The request of King George was bitterly opposed in the Dutch Congress by Baron Van der Capellen and other political opponents of the stadholder and by friends of the Americans. In the West Indies, the Dutch governor Johannes de Graaf showed open sympathy with our fathers. On the 16th of November, 1776, he ordered the first foreign salute fired to the flag of the United States of America. King George at last secured about thirty thousand Hessians to do his vile work in America.

Since the British ships captured all American vessels they could find, and treated their crews with great cruelty, the people of the colonies, slowly but surely, became united in a desire for independence. Indeed, they soon began to feel that they would obtain it if they should fight for it.

There was also great sympathy with the American cause in France and Germany. Besides Lafayette, the Frenchman; De Kalb and Steuben, Germans; Kosciusko and Pulaski, Poles; Romans and Dirck, Dutchmen, — there were other European officers who crossed the ocean to help our fathers.

In Philadelphia there was an Englishman, Thomas Paine, who had emigrated from the eastern counties where nonconformity had always been so strong, whence most of the emigrants to New England had come and in which the parliamentary armies had been mostly raised. Paine was a literary man, editor, and clerk of the Pennsylvania Assembly, and all his life an unselfish champion of the rights of man. He wrote a pamphlet called " Common Sense," in which he declared that the time had come for a final separation from England, and that arms must decide the contest. This little pamphlet voiced the sentiment of thousands and tens of thousands of people who were thinking the same thoughts. It was the most widely circulated and most generally read document yet printed in America.

When the Continental Congress met again in Philadelphia in June, 1776, it was no longer one of colonies only. Some of these had already become states. In North Carolina, as we read on the state seal to-day, the people of Mecklenburg County, mostly Scotch-Irish, had, on May 30, 1775, declared their independence, and on April 12, 1776, the provincial Congress instructed their delegates to Philadelphia to vote for separation from Great Britain. The motion to become a nation came from the oldest of the colonies, and the seconding from the next in age and dignity. Richard Henry Lee, of Virginia, offered a resolution that " these united colonies are and of right ought to be free and independent states." John Adams, of Massachusetts, seconded the resolution.

The committee of five to prepare the declaration consisted of Thomas Jefferson, John Adams, Benjamin Franklin, Roger Sherman, and Robert Livingston. The document was the work of Thomas Jefferson, and was written by him in a house on the corner of Seventh and Market streets. After being debated in the State House, in the room now called Independence Hall, it was signed on the 4th of July by John Hancock, president of the Congress. It was read in Independence Square to the people, from a timber stand or observatory which had been erected for Rittenhouse to observe the transit of Venus, which took place on June 3, 1769. In the view of the world a new luminary was passing across the great disc of history on July 4, 1776.

Then the "old liberty bell" was rung in the State House. In Massachusetts the name of the town with the highest altitude in the state was changed from "Gage" to "Washington." In New York city the people tore down the leaden statue of King George and melted the lead into bullets. The name of Tryon County was changed to that of Montgomery. Later divisions were called after Americans, — Herkimer, Madison, Fulton, and Hamilton.

When the representatives of the thirteen colonies added their names to the immortal Declaration, the work of severance, preparatory to a "more perfect union" of the "people of the United States," was done. Our nation came into existence and the colonial era of our history was over. Like the Dutch republic, our thirteen states, protesting against illegal taxation, first formed a federal union, keeping up government in the name of the king, and then, in the month of July, declared themselves independent and entered as a sovereign nation upon the war which resulted in freedom under law. Our country borrowed most of her political precedents from the free republic of the Netherlands, while reinforcing and safeguarding the organism with the noblest British precedents. The romance of American colonization had become the reality of the United States of America.